Dragons Die at Dawn

A mystery novel

Dragons Die at Dawn

A mystery novel

by
William M. Davenport

Thanks for your interest
in my humble pages.
Best wishes,
William M. Davenport
Sept. 21, 2001

ISBN: 1-58820-122-8

1stBooks – rev. 10/13/00

Prologue

George King's locomotive exploded at four a.m. August 9, 1941, near the eastern North Carolina town of Fallston. The person who planned the explosion believed that he would get away with murder if the blast looked like an accident, especially if it appeared to have been caused by the carelessness of the locomotive's dead crew. The killer's main concern was the possibility of witnesses. The murderer knew that there would be a fifty-fifty chance that the locomotive would stop near a cluster of tobacco barns located near the track. He also knew that since tobacco was being harvested from the fields nearby, although the town would be sleeping, someone would necessarily be at the curing barns throughout the night. So the resourceful killer had a contingency plan: Use the witness or kill him.

The village of Fallston was once a lively, thriving river port. Likewise, the tobacco barns at the scene of the explosion were located on what was once a much larger, more prosperous plantation. At the time of the tragedy, however, both town and river farm were so forlorn and run-down that dogs living in and around them had all but forgotten how to bark.

Fallston's port lights no longer beamed and its fog horns no longer sounded mournfully to warn boats passing along the misty Roanoke River. That dark night, the Roanoke's sea-bound waters reached the vicinity of the river barns before any sign of humanity marked its journey. The fire from the barns' furnaces managed to send feeble flickers of red light across the stream, creating the illusion that Roanoke's waters were the color of dried blood.

The trio of River Barns were built at ninety-degree intervals on the outer perimeter of a half-circle with a radius of fifty feet. The firebox of each of the barn's furnaces pointed toward the circle's midpoint. A makeshift T-shaped tin roof measuring ten feet across connected each barn at the center of that circle. Wooden poles supported the shelter. This structure which had no walls, wasn't much, but it did provide some protection from sun and rain. It was there that Frank Ruffin and Jubal Scott had assimilated many of the comforts of home: cots, chairs, pillows, a table, blankets, lanterns, food, water and Ruffin's notorious alarm clock. Plus, the pair had all outdoors for a toilet.

Tobacco curing barns built before 1941 were not built for looks. Unskilled farm laborers using home-grown material constructed the singe-purpose, ugly twenty-foot square cubes. The barns had dirt floors and were built without the benefit of a foundation. The earthen floor contained the furnace and a connected network of round metal ducts or flues from which flue cured tobacco got its name.

Tobacco barns were notorious fire traps, perhaps the most unsafe and unlikely ovens ever built. From the farmers' viewpoint, however, barns could be built with excess labor and materials and with a little luck would last throughout the six-week curing season. Barn burnings were so common that the structures were built in isolated places far from other buildings. At the river farm, the nearest building to the river barns was about a half-mile away. There was an unwritten law that neighbors could count on each other if one of their barns caught on fire during the harvest season.

Chapter 1: The Ninety and Nine Crew

August 8, 1941 was one of the hottest days of the year, a day the likes of which a Carolina Chamber of Commerce would never mention. Days of that sort demanded the most from the flue-cured tobacco farmer. Continued exposure to the sun on such days would ripen and rot tobacco while it was still on the stalk. That situation would leave the farmer an unpleasant choice: Chance a heat stroke and get the tobacco out of the sun, or stay in the shade and watch his money crop rot in the field. The good news about the predawn hours of August 9, however, was that the grueling six-week tobacco harvesting season was nearing its end. Only the smallest, topmost leaves were left on the tobacco plants in the field.

Here and there in the nearby fields, selected plants had paper bags jammed over their seed heads. These seed bag crowns were reserved for the farm's tallest, healthiest tobacco plants, some more than six feet tall. Heavy string was tied snugly around the neck of each inverted sack to keep the tiny precious seeds from falling out. In about a week the harvesting season would be over. The collection of seeds that followed would signal that farmers were already preparing for the next year.

In the eerie moonlight to which the boy had become accustomed, he often imagined that the stripped tobacco stalks were aliens on the attack led by the taller ones crowned by paper bags. By day, however, in the stark, shimmering sunlight, the sacked plants reminded the nine-year-old of naked old men stripped of everything but their hats. Although Jubal Scott never admitted this to anyone, the bagged plants actually reminded him of one old man in particular. That man was his beloved "Uncle Frank" Ruffin. Advancing age stripped away much of Frank Ruffin's vitality and agility. As Jubal's father selected and crowned the finest of his tobacco plants, Jubal subconsciously felt that he was honoring Frank Ruffin. Jubal was replanting in his own mind the richest, most productive grains of wisdom transcended to him from his relationship with the old man. To complete the analogy, everyone from miles around knew that

Frank Ruffin would never be seen, dead or alive, in public without his hat.

With the exception of Mason Scott, Jubal's father, all the farmers around rotated overnight curing duties with their able-bodied men, a chore that always came after a sixteen-hour, back-breaking day. Every farmhand knew that a sleepyhead tending one or more barns was an invitation to disaster. But this risk was taken collectively without complaint. Everyone involved knew that farming itself was a gamble and that paying outside labor was a sure-fire way to lose money.

Oddly, Mason Scott decided to assign not one, but two full-time people to do his night curing. However, this was not the seemingly extravagant act that it appeared to be; Mason Scott was gambling, too. He was betting that two halves would make a whole, even when the halves happened to be very, very different.

Uncle Frank Ruffin, as everyone on the farm called him, was black and admittedly "ever day o' ninety," while Jubal Early Scott was white and boasted of "goin on ten." When Jubal's father, the farm's overseer wasn't around, Frank Ruffin and Jubal Scott were jokingly called the Mister Scott's Ninety and Nine Crew. Everyone on the Sweetwater Farm knew that the odd pairing was the boss' idea. They also knew that the boss man didn't think the Ninety and Nine title was funny.

During those days Mason Scott didn't think anything was funny. For his part, Uncle Frank was ambivalent toward the Ninety and Nine joke, but Jubal loved everything about it, the title, the job and especially the extra attention. By his own assessment, Frank Ruffin had a mind that was tolerably keen, had knees that were next to no good and eyesight that was middling to poor. The boy's job was to be Uncle Frank's arms, legs and eyes. Jubal believed that the formation of the Ninety and Nine Crew was one of the most brilliant moves his father made since becoming overseer at the Roanoke River farm.

Around midnight, a powerful electrical storm provided the pair with a spectacular sound and light show. While the storm raged, the boy's head just happened to be buried deep beneath his pillow. Well after the thunder subsided, Jubal eased his pillow aside and began to enjoy the sweet music of rain striking the barn shelter's rusty tin roof. This pleasant sensation was sweetened as a cooling mist penetrated the air that surrounded him. Above the soothing din, the boy could hear the voice of Frank Ruffin as he prayed aloud, thanking "de good Lawd" for sending the storm and the rain.

When the old man finished praying, Jubal said, "I heard you praying for the rain just then. But you thanked God for the storm, too. Why would you thank God for a thing like that? Don't you realize that both of us could have been killed?"

"Sho, I know dat fo sho. But, we won't killed, wus we?"

"You didn't understand my question, Uncle Frank," the boy argued. My question is, why did God send the storm in the first place? I sure didn't ask for anything like that. Did you?"

It was customary in those days for southern white children to refer to elderly black people as Aunt or Uncle.

"Naw, boy, I didn't fur hit, but I'm a'praisin' de Lawd fur sendin' it."

"Why in the world do you want to do that?"

"Cause God was a'teachin' both of us somethin' wid dat storm, if'n we'ze got de ears to heah and eyes dat see."

"Well, now we're finally getting somewhere. Supposen you tell me 'xactly what God was a'wantin' us to hear and see."

"De good Lawd was a'showin' us a little speck of his mighty power wid dat storm. He wus a'teachin' us how he's gone take care of us when other kinds of bad storms comes long. Yo is right boy, dat lightin' won't nuthin to play wid. De Lawd coulda' burned us up like Sodom and Gomorrah if he wus a mind to. But he didn't. So you sees, dat's why I praises him fo' his mighty storms just de same as fo his sweet rain."

"Won't you scared of the thunder and lightning?"

"Sho, I was. But I knowed God won't gone send no storm to yo Uncle Frank lessen he need hit. Lawd Jesus use dem storms to show me who he am and who I is. Yo ole Uncle Frank need some showin' like dat ever now and den."

After that exchange, much of which was lost on the boy, the pair became quiet again. Area crickets, frogs and a host of unidentified critters took up the praise theme with a symphony of

3

their own. Hours ago the sultry air in the area was as dead as lead. Now joyful croaks, groans and chirps filled the air around them. Unfortunately, as often happens in the very midst of purest joy and contentment, Satan was standing in the wings, waiting for a chance to deal some cards of his own.

Lulled by the combination of coolness and pleasant smells around him, Jubal was about to indulge himself with a short nap. It was three a.m. according to Frank Ruffin's notorious alarm clock. The dreaded noisy ticker, appearing to be squatting on its spraddled legs, was facing a lighted kerosene lamp. The lantern and clock sat atop a table made of rough planks that had been lain across a pair of wobbly castoff sawhorses. On one side of the makeshift table Jubal Early Scott rested on his rickety cot. The nine-year-old looked sleepily across the table at an old man in his nineties. Frank Ruffin swayed gently to and fro in a cane-bottomed rocking chair.

Alternating light and shadow emanating from the nearby tobacco barn furnaces added romance to the idyllic scene. The pungent odors of drying, dying tobacco leaves combined with the wood smoke were strong enough to keep the mosquitoes away and powerful enough to enhance the dreaminess and sleepiness of man and boy. The serenity and quiescence of the village projected the idea that the population of Fallston would continue sleeping for at least the next several hours.

Opiates in the air engulfing the river barns also indicated that the old man and the boy would soon join the citizens of Fallston in their sonorous pursuits. Contrary to appearances, however, nothing could have been further from the truth. Within the hour the explosion would occur. That blast will shake Fallston's dead, wake their living, and change young Jubal Scott's life forever.

Frank Ruffin began to hum. It was the old man's way of fighting sleep. Jubal Scott's eyes were closed, and he let his mind drift into the message and words of the old man's familiar melody. The boy's near-out-of-mind experience was suggesting to him that he might have been as near heaven at that very moment as he would ever be again. The old man's thoughts were along the same line. But unlike the boy, Frank Ruffin knew with certainty that a grand and glorious new Fallston was waiting

4

for him in paradise. Heavenly thoughts aside, the languid scene begged a more timely question: How did such an odd, dreamy, distracted pair become entrusted with the money crop that five families were depending on for their very survival? Appearances and questions aside, the two had performed together flawlessly for forty-three nights: sundown to sunup, at the dangerous, isolated site without a single night off.

With the help of his mammoth alarm clock, Uncle Frank religiously kept the two on a ten-minute schedule. Jubal thought the old man had the biggest, loudest, meanest alarm clock in the world. Just when he was on the verge of dozing, he heard the faraway, yet unmistakable sound of a steam locomotive whistle. He pushed up on his elbows and listened. Jubal needed to make sure that he wasn't dreaming before sharing such a wild conclusion with Uncle Frank. The sound repeated. The second sound could have been an echo. Sometimes when the air is heavy after a shower, sounds reverberate in the gullies near the river. But echo or not, there was no doubt that the steam locomotive whistle was real.

"I didn't know a train ever came here at night."

"Like I say, hit's a special," Uncle Frank responded. Most old people repeat themselves, but Frank Ruffin often displayed the curious habit of merely claiming to do so.

"Do you really think the train's coming here?"

Dumb question. Uncle Frank jumped on it.

"Sho, hit'sa comin' heah. Whar else do you think hit's qwine go, New Yauk City maybe? Nah, boy, I'ze fraid deah ain't no other place fer hit to get to but right heah where we'ze a sittin'."

Stung by his own stupidity, the boy countered by observing, "Well, at last it sounds like we're about to have a little action around this dead place."

"Whut yo a'runnin' on' bout now, boy?"

The boy was being facetious. But his statement was also true. Nothing more exciting than the pulpwood train's arrival by moonlight had happened around Fallston in a long, long time. Every citizen for miles around knew that the pulpwood train always arrived in Fallston between ten in the morning and high noon every Monday, Wednesday and Friday. Changes of this magnitude made big, big news around a place like Fallston.

True or not, Frank Ruffin did not take well to put-downs of his beloved Fallston. Jubal knew that he could forget his nap now. He was in for one of Uncle Frank's lectures of the good old glory days of Fallston.

Chapter 2: The Locomotive Crew

Flagman Lacy Brandon acknowledged the lantern signal from the conductor, and George King opened the throttle. Moments later their train was lumbering through the sleeping town of Martin North Carolina. The stop in Martin was to drop off an empty boxcar at the Perry Peanut Processing Plant. Only a dozen empty flatcars and a caboose followed engine 608. The empties were to be swapped for an equal number of flatcars loaded with pulpwood that were waiting for them at Fallston.

The night run of a pulpwood train to Fallston was a first. For twenty years, the pulpwood train made its daylight runs to Fallston three days each week. But of late the railroad had been hard pressed to keep up with overwhelming demands for its services. The accelerating war in Europe created an ever-expanding market for American goods and supplies. There was also a corresponding surge in the railroad's business. This welcome boom followed a decade of steady decline and cutbacks in the demand for railroad services. Evidence of the lean years, better known as the Great Depression, was seen everywhere along the pulpwood run. The fifty miles of track between Centerville and Fallston were littered with boarded-up and abandoned depots, weeds, branch lines and side tracks leading to nowhere. Before the Depression, passengers could travel by rail to almost any town or village in the eastern part of the state.

The Fallston pulpwood run marked a bitter-sweet reunion for George King, Lacy Brandon and Jim Spencer. These men had not worked together since that trio got themselves tangled up in a tragic accident more than a year ago. That accident happened when a yard engine, manned by this crew, moved a standing passenger coach, and in the process crushed and killed the pipefitter working beneath it. While the direct cause of that accident was never clearly determined, blame, scorn, hatred, and finally demotion were heaped upon the three-man crew of the shop yard locomotive.

The placement and removal of worker's flags was one of the most sacred and strictly enforced regulations in the railroad rule

7

book. Before working beneath any standing railroad car located outside of a closed shop or building, a worker was required to place flags identifying himself and his craft at each end of the standing car or string of cars. Nobody other than the worker who set the craftsman's flags had the authority to remove them. If a craftsman left work without removing his flags, and the company wanted to move a flagged unit, the foreman had to send for that workman. That craftsman and only that craftsman could remove those particular flags. Proven violations of flag rules often resulted in dismissal, and criminal charges had been known to apply.

In the afore-mentioned accident of a year ago, Harry Collins was crushed to death beneath the wheels of the car under which he was working. The cause of his death was ultimately listed as accidental.

Harry Collins' supervisor and peers considered him to be one of the most competent, safety-minded workers in the Centerville Railroad Shops. A properly placed flag was found standing at the opposite end of the car at the time of the accident. Several shop workers testified that they had seen the other properly placed flag ten minutes prior to the accident. That second flag, however, was not found. The lack of hard evidence did little to placate the angry shop workers. Throughout the sprawling railroad shops, scorn, anger, suspicion and even death threats were heaped upon the yard engine crew.

The brunt of the shopmen's fury fell on Lacy Brandon, who was the switchman in charge of the yard engine crew that fateful day. The railroad investigators and labor unions did their best to settle the matter peaceably. However, in the end, investigators failed to establish culpability for the death of Harry Collins. The dead man's widow was quickly awarded fifty thousand dollars, a sizable fortune for that time. That generous award, however, did little toward ending the matter.

Tension ran so high following the death of Harry Collins that the company finally decided that for their own safety, the yard crew could no longer work inside the Centerville Shops. The crew's unions put up a fight, but the three crewmen were ultimately relegated, according to their respective crafts, to the lowest rung of new seniority rosters, collectively know as "extra boards." The loss of seniority soured the crew. Extra Boards were made up of trainmen without sufficient seniority to stand for a regular run.   Extra boarders seldom knew until the last moment when they would be scheduled to work.

The apparent demotion of the crew, however, soon turned into a financial asset. In good times, the extra board was the place to be. And these were good times. In addition to normal relief work, extra boarders were called upon to staff the spate of new and special runs cropping up daily. The crew of 608 was making more money than the regulars.

George King and Jim Spencer were aware that talking about the flag incident could be difficult for Lacy. Therefore, George and Jim, out of respect for their friend, agreed between themselves not to mention the subject unless Brandon brought it up. Oddly enough, Lacy Brandon was thinking the very same thing. "Why bring up that sad subject," he was thinking. "These guys stuck by me through a very difficult ordeal. I'm sure they don't want to rehash all that pain and misery."

An hour passed. The 608 crossed the Green County line. Now it was more than half way to its destination, and so far there had been no mention of the flag incident. The three were enjoying each other's company, but inwardly each was dying to talk about the Collins case.

"Shall I wake Fallston up when we get there?" King chided while blowing the whistle for the highway crossing just outside of Martin.

"Nah, let em' sleep.   Let those country hayseeds think somebody stole their pulpwood during the night," Spencer countered.

The flag subject hiatus held until they were out of Martin and well on the way to Fallston when suddenly Spencer shouted above the squeaking and grinding of 608, "Hey, Lace, you make damn sure there ain't no tree cutter's flag set on dem pulpwood cars we're pickin' up in Fallston."

Spencer's thoughtless remark was meant to be a joke, but nobody laughed. The fireman immediately regretted bringing up

9

the subject, but now that the awkward self-imposed gag rule was broken, everybody wanted to talk.

George King now felt free to ask Brandon the question that he'd been harboring all evening. However, he prefaced it by reporting, "Just last week I accidentally met two of those shop goons on the street. They threatened to kill me if they ever saw me in another shop engine. From what I hear, crap like that is probably mild to the stuff you've had thrown at you. How in the world have you kept from going crazy, Lace? Have those bastards at the shops let up on you yet?"

"If it wasn't for my faith in the good Lord, my wife, good people at my church, and friends like you guys, I would never have made it this far, that's for sure. But it hasn't been so bad lately. I've gotten only one threatening letter and a couple of phone calls so far this month. I can live with a nasty letter or a phone call once in a while. For a time there I was getting letters and packages almost every day. You wouldn't believe some of the things in the packages people mailed to me. How has it been with you lately, Jim?"

"I got a few nasty phone calls early on, and a whole lotta mean looks, but no one ever wrote me any threatening letters or sent me any crap in the mail," Spencer answered. "I don't think I'd a' been able to put up with all the garbage you've been through, Lacy."

"You said something about your church. Aren't there a lot of those railroad shop workers right there in your church, Lace? How do you get along with them?"

"Yeah, there are some. And I'm getting along with them just fine. But there aren't near as many of them now as there was when this flag business first happened."

"It's a wonder they didn't kick your butt right out of the church," Spencer countered.

"You're right, Spence, that is a wonder."

"What do you mean by that, Lace?" King queried.

"It was really bad there for awhile. Just like Jim said, a lot of the members wanted me out of the church," Brandon responded. "In fact it got so bad that people who thought I was innocent sat on one side of the church, and those who thought I

10

was guilty sat on the other. I offered to leave. The last thing I wanted was to see the church split like that. But my pastor and most of the deacons kept on encouraging me to stay. Instead of calming down, things just got worse and worse. Finally, one Sunday morning, when things were at their very worst, my pastor announced straight out, right from the pulpit, that any member who believed that I was guilty or lying about my part in the death of Harry Collins should find themselves another church. Half of the congregation got up and walked out right then and there. For a couple of months our attendance was down, but praise the Lord, since then we have been gaining new members. Our church has actually grown since the death of Harry Collins. It was all by the grace of my Lord Jesus that things have worked out so well. Romans 8:28 says that all things work together for those who love the lord. I believe that with all my hea--a--r-t."

"Those goof balls in the shops must have really believed that we hid that damn flag," Spencer interrupted. The fireman was becoming less and less at ease. He liked and respected Lacy Brandon, but he simply couldn't stand Brandon's or anyone else's preaching. "George and me watched you walk right up to the drawhead on that car, Lace. If there'd been a damn flag, all three of us would'a seen it. And you'd a' broke your fool leg stumbling over the blasted thing. I guess those pipe benders finally decided that we ate the damn thing."

George King put the subject in practical terms when he said, "As soon as the news that Harry Collins was dead got out in those shops that day, there were men swarming all over the cab of my engine. They even made me get up while they looked under my seat, for God's sake. And remember those two guys that crawled into the water tender? All that pair got for their trouble was a two-inch coating of rusty slime from the bottom of the tank."

Jim Spencer was now laughing so hard that his cap fell off. When he recovered his red polka-dot trademark he joined in with, "And two of the bastards raked all the coal out of my hopper. They even brought one of their Go...., er, da.. blasted flags into the cab and tried to shove th' son o' bi..... er... darn,

11

thing into the fire box, but it was too wide and wouldn't go." Jim Spencer knew that Lacy Brandon neither used nor appreciated profanity. Realizing this, Jim obviously struggled to tone down his normally profane pattern of speech.

Lacy Brandon knew that Jim Spencer was an anti-church person. Something in the feisty fireman's background must have soured him against all forms of organized religion. Lacy Brandon knew that preaching was not the best way to witness to Jim Spencer. Yet he was not willing to give up, so he continued, "Like you say, Jim, those people really believed that we did away with that flag. I feel sorry for people who can't or won't accept the truth."

"Are you saying that I don't see the truth about God and church and all that religious stuff you preach about, Lace?" Spencer's hackles were up.

"No, no, Jim, please don't misunderstand me. I'm not judging you or anyone else. I'm simply saying that everyone is entitled and free to make up his or her own mind. Many people right here in Centerville sincerely believe that we did away with that flag. In spite of the fact that the three of us know that they are dead wrong, those people are entitled to their own opinions."

"Yeah, I think I see that now. You're saying that the truth is the truth whether you or I or anyone else believes it or not. Isn't that what you're saying, Lace?"

"Yep. That's exactly what I was trying to say. Only you said it much better that I could have, Jim," Brandon responded.

"Hey. Yeah! Maybe I'd better have a talk to that preacher of yours. Sounds to me like he's a man who believes what he says and does something about what he believes."

"Hey, preacher boys. You'd better be gettin' your minds off all those beautiful theories and onto some real ugly pulpwood cars," George King reminded his crew. All three were laughing heartily as George King gave his whistle cord several lusty yanks as 608 approached the Fallston cut-off road. Moments later the reunited, laughing crew were swaying and chugging their merry way around the sleepy town of Fallston.

12

Chapter 3: The Killer

A mile from the river barns, two men in an automobile anxiously awaited the arrival of the Fallston pulpwood train. They had parked their car in a secluded spot. Without fear of being detected, the pair had a clear view of the railroad track as well as the single road leading into and out of the town of Fallston. One of the men was watching with dread and trepidation as the train passed. He wanted to do the job he had already been paid to do and get it over with. The other man viewed the pulpwood train as an opportunity. He had planned well; all the pieces were finally falling into place. The motive, however, for the killer's impending homicidal act had not been truthfully shared with his partner in crime. That truth would have sickened and depressed the killer's hapless accomplice even more.

By the early 1800s, Fallston had become a thriving river port. By the late 1800s, the railroad wanted in on the booming business there. The railroad wanted to lay their tracks on a direct line to the port. This meant that the track would have to pass between a row of the finest mansions in eastern North Carolina. The rich mansion owners resisted this plan. In the end, the railroad gave in and built a track that looped around the town. The compromise turned out to be convenient for both parties. The mansions were spared, and trains arriving in Fallston could head into town and head out, with the flip of a switch.

Just as he was about to start his engine, the driver of the car spotted headlights approaching their direction. Any traffic on that lonely road at three in the morning would be cause for concern. This surprising turn of events became even more surprising when the car turned out to be a late-model chauffeur-driven limousine. Luckily for the driver of the parked car, he had not turned on his headlights. The pair in the hidden car watched anxiously as the limo passed and continued to make its way down Center Street. Without the benefit of headlights, the driver moved his car to a spot where they could watch the limousine. The big car glided into the driveway of one of the large mansions that lined Fallston's main avenue. The men waited until both the limo and porch lights at the mansion were extinguished.

"Let's sit here a few minutes more. We'll let the rich bastards in that house settle down. We've got plenty of time," the smaller man snapped.

"You told me we wouldn't see nobody in this town. Everybody would be asleep you said," the driver whined.

"Shut up and leave the worrying to me. The people in that house don't have a damn thing to do with our business. In no time that stuffed shirt will be asleep like all the other clods in this dump. We're gonna wake up this whole damn countryside about forty-five minutes from now. But, by the time they figure out what has happened, we'll be way th' hell away from here."

The driver stared anxiously down the now dark street as he waited for orders. The other man appeared to be perfectly composed as he savored the moment. He, too, was celebrating the reunion of the missing flag crew.

Feeling the need to vindicate himself, the big man said, "That stupid engine crew is going to get exactly what they deserve, ain't they? An eye for an eye and a tooth for a tooth that's what I always say. They killed my friend Harry, didn't they? Harry Collins was a fine man. I was Harry's helper for more than a year. He was real particular about all kinds of safety rules, and most especially fussy about settin' flags. He'd let me put the flags out for him, but he'd always check for himself to see if they were right where he wanted them. Those cocky s.o.b.s' moved that flag and killed my friend. Now, they're gonna get just what they deserve. Just what they gave poor Harry Collins. Ain't that right?"

"That's exactly what they did." Happy now for a chance to placate his nervous helper, the little man continued, "And then the cheap bastards didn't have guts enough to admit it. Right now I'll bet you they're laughing their stupid heads off. But we've got news for them, haven't we? They're not going to get away with killing our friend, not by a long shot." The pep talk helped, but what the big man needed even more was a snort from the bottle now hidden under his pant leg. And, pretending to

14

scratch, he checked to make sure that his precious flask was still there.

Finally the boss said, "Let's go." The driver made his way slowly around Fallston's Circle Drive in the opposite direction from the pulpwood train of five minutes earlier. Actually their southern route had been dictated by the northern route of the pulpwood train. The killer knew that the locomotive of the pulpwood train would stop in the vicinity of the river barns. Another frustrating surprise, however, cropped up as the car reached the spot where their intended route took them away from the town's circle road. They had planned to drive by moonlight to the track side without the use of headlights. But a thick cumulus cloud positioned its fat self squarely in the line of sight between the moon and the path to which the pair were committed.

"Hell, I can't see a damn thing. I've never been down this path before. We're going to wind up in a ditch. If that happens, we'll never get outta here."

"You're right. Damn that rain. It gets muddy down there awful fast. Turn your lights back on and let's get down there as quick as we can." The killer was using a small pen light to check the time. "The locomotive won't be here for another five minutes at the earliest."

With headlights glowing, the car quickly bumped its way down the muddy, rutty narrow lane. The car's lights were needed until they reached the predetermined parking spot. The lights were also left on while the driver turned the car around and positioned it for the getaway. As he got out of the car, the big man noticed that barn fires were glowing on the rise opposite the tracks. This meant potential witnesses. Happiness replaced the big man's dread. The job was about to be called off. Witnesses? Yes. Job. No. That had been their bargain all along. The driver jumped back into the car and was about to start the engine when he felt something hard pressing against his upper torso. The smaller man reached across and grabbed the key with one hand, and with the other was poking the barrel of a pistol into the big man's ribs.

"Now you listen to me and you listen good." The tone of the smaller man's voice was very compelling. "I knew there was a chance that somebody might be at those barns. I wouldn't expect someone as dumb as you to think of that. But not a damn thing's changed. You're going to do exactly like I say. This job is going to get done just the way I planned it or you'll be the one found dead instead of those three railroad monkeys. You listen to me and do exactly what I tell you to do. Do you understand?"

"I understand, but I don't like it. What if the man curing tobacco comes over here and sees what we're doing?"

"I ain't got time to argue with you. We've got work to do. One hour from now we'll both be out of this jerk water town forever. And we'll be in the clear. Now, here's what I want you to do."

Chapter 4: The Limousine

Ostensibly, Callie Parsons had gone to New York City on a buying trip for her general store. Her real purpose, however, was to visit a neurosurgeon. Only Callie Parsons' trusted house servants and personal attorney knew about the deadly time bomb ticking away in the middle of her brain. She reached Centerville on the streamliner just after midnight. Edward, her butler, chauffeur and handy man met her at the Centerville station. Because of a delay with the luggage, it was very late by the time they reached Fallston. Near Fallston, as her limousine passed the pulpwood train, Edward commented that this was the first time he'd seen the pulpwood, or any other train for that matter, in this part of the country at this time of night.

Miss Parsons answered, "The railroad company notified me a couple of weeks back that something like this might happen. Because of the war, the railroad, like everybody else, is swamped with business these days. The railroad company told me last week that they're having to do a lot of shuffling in order to satisfy all their customers. If I had only known the pulpwood train was headed this way tonight, I could have hitched a ride in the caboose, and you could have stayed home."

Edward laughed. And the joke ended the conversation. But Miss Parsons, who owned controlling interest in the pulpwood company, was glad to know that the railroad meant business when they assured her that they would continue to meet their commitment of three pulpwood runs each week.

Once inside her mansion, Callie Parsons went directly to her upstairs bedroom. She was very tired. To be sure she would say her prayers before falling asleep, she was petitioning the lord while changing into her nightgown. Before reaching her much desired bed, she noticed that her bedroom window had been closed. "Mildred must have closed the window. We must have had some rain while I was away," she said to herself. She recrossed the room and opened the window opposite her bed. The fresh air issued an instant and pleasant reward. She began talking to herself again when she spotted a car slowly making its way around Circle Drive.

"This is good," she said. "The railroad is sending a man down to make sure that my pulpwood gets properly loaded. Those people really know how to take care of their business and mine." But as she watched, the car surprised her by turning into a small path and then disappearing into the woods.

"Now, what can anyone be doing down there at this time of the morning? There's nothing down there but chiggers, snakes, ticks and the railroad track. Lovers, I guess," she said out loud. Lately Callie Parsons had taken to talking to herself. She took her new habit in stride, thinking that this must be yet another sign of her advancing age.

Callie Parsons was probably the wealthiest woman in the county. She was also one of the most respected. As a young woman, Callie was seriously on her way to realizing her dream of becoming a trial lawyer. But a distress signal from her mother brought her back home to Fallston. As an only child, Callie left school temporarily to help out when her father was suddenly stricken and disabled by a stroke. Following his death a year later, her mother needed her at home to put the family's business affairs in order.

The Parsons owned almost half of the county's farmland and considerable other holdings, including the general store in Fallston. Parsons' General Store was the emporium that was keeping the town alive. Its continuing success was not difficult to understand. Parsons' tenant farmers virtually lived off "the store" from January until harvest-time.

Just as young Callie was packing for her return to law school at Chapel Hill, her mother became ill. Again the mother asked Callie to remain at home. "Just for a while, until I get on my feet," her mother had said. That "while" turned out to be twenty more years. By the time her mother died, Callie Parsons had become a very rich and highly successful business woman. She never married, and claimed she knew every eligible man for miles around and would have no part of the lot.

Ordinarily the wayward car would not have bothered Callie. But these were not ordinary times. She learned just hours before

18

that the aneurysm in her head could burst at any moment. The size and location of the giant bubble ruled out any chance of operating, and neither treatment nor medication would help. Not if, but when that bubble bursts Callie Parsons' life on earth would be over.

Lately Callie Parsons had been petitioning God that he might let her realize the one lifelong dream that had thus far eluded her. Even as she prayed, however, she realized that her prayer was a selfish one. Wasn't seventy-plus years of good health and wealth enough? Nevertheless, her prayer persisted and would not go away. And there, in the pitch blackness of her room Callie Parsons realized that God could be sending her a message. A pale haze of light was visible above the tree line. As Callie Parsons' eyes became adjusted, that weak halo of light, the supplicant noticed, was a pink aura rising up from the earth somewhere beyond the tracks. And as she watched the blending of this phenomenon a feeling of peace and wonder washed over her entire body. She knows now that God was answering her prayer. She knew that she would be given a role in solving a murder case.

After a long, long day, Callie Parsons was soon not only at peace; the woman was snoring.

Chapter 5: The Locomotive

For the next ten minutes the boy was transcended to another time and seemingly another place. Actually, the boy didn't mind. Frank Ruffin was a master storyteller. And as the old man talked, his rich, even voice painted the scenes. Figuratively, the boy was transported back in time from the present all but abandoned, forlorn town of Fallston. Gradually, as the old man spoke, the dead town became its former vibrant self, replete with color, sounds, sights and smells. As Frank Ruffin intoned, the river shacks and shanties were transformed into bright colorful shops and bustling beehives of activity. The river and town were soon teeming with boats, trains, wagons and people of every sort: Gamblers, traders, merchants, show men, evangelists and hucksters all pedaling their wares on the popular streets of Fallston. In his dreamy state, Jubal listened for the sounds of the town band playing in the park on a summer Sunday afternoon. The Grand Hotel and magnificent mansions along Main Street were magically awash with grandeur as the rich of Fallston wined, dined, danced and played their evening away.

Suddenly, always suddenly, the clock sounded its alarm and the two went back to the solitary tobacco patch.

Two of the three river barns were currently being fired, and only those required the Ninety and Nine's attention. The crude barn furnaces were made of home-baked bricks from Roanoke River red clay. The fire chambers were built roughly in the shape of an igloo door and positioned half in and half out of the barns. As a precautionary measure to prevent a wood barn from burning, half of the furnace was actually inside the barn. Although there were no standards, a typical furnace's "igloo" would measure roughly eight feet from end to end. The outside, open-ended half of the igloo contained the fire. Slabs of sawmill scraps, small limbs, and cut timber were stacked by each of the barns. The work of gathering and stacking wood for curing was done during the slack season of winter.

The half that extended into the barn was connected to a network of large metal flues that ringed the barn floor. Finally, smaller, vertical risers were attached to the flues at critical points. These dual-purpose risers acted as chimney and heater for the area of the barn through which they passed. Together with the ring of floor flues, the riser vents guaranteed an even draft throughout the barn's interior.

"Which barn do you want to see about first?" Jubal asked.

"Let's check on dat raisin' barn fust."

Jubal read and reported the temperature in the raising barn to Uncle Frank. Determining that the temperature needed to be raised, Uncle Frank ordered Jubal to throw fresh wood into the furnace. As Jubal was stoking the raising barn's furnace, he could tell by the sound of the engine that the train had entered the loop and was now circling Fallston in a clockwise direction. The town of Fallston was built on a part of a large cul-de-sac, around which the river bends. The farm on which the Scotts and Uncle Frank lived made up the balance of that isolated tract of land. The location of Fallston was a perfect spot for a river port, with a sweeping view of the river and lots of prime riverfront property. But that uniqueness ultimately became the cause of the town's death. Since the 1920s, new highways and the burgeoning roadway trucking industry combined to make Fallston an unnecessary and out-of-the-way place.

During Fallston's halcyon river-port days, the railroad built a track around the town so its trains could head in and head out without undue switching. The town loop afforded the pulpwood train crew to enter town from either direction. The route they took meant that the shifting would take place in the vicinity of the river barns. Jubal was happy about that. He would be close to the action, and as it turned out, closer to more action than he could have imagined.

By the time the boy reached the door to the "killing heat" barn, Uncle Frank was already there. The boy's thoughts were more on the train than tobacco, and accordingly had dallied along the way. Uncle Frank never let Jubal enter a killing heat barn without being with him. As Jubal tugged at the insulated bags to open the heavy door, he couldn't miss the point that the bags were very hot. This was the moment of maximum danger. If a fire were to be smoldering inside, the opening of the door would cause an immediate explosion of flame and heat. That blast would be aimed directly at the open doorway. Jubal's attention returned to the business at hand.

Once the door was safely opened, the boy had to be both quick and careful. His first hurdle was to clear the big flue pipe just inside the door without touching it. Contact with this pipe would mean instant pain and a long lasting blister. To avoid this he had to jump from the door frame to a spot beyond the first flue into the pitch black interior of the curing oven. The trick was to make sure he stopped before bumping into the next flue. Uncle Frank had been holding the lantern and a tobacco stick until the boy was safely inside. Jubal reached over and took them now. He quickly noted that the thermometers were reading almost one hundred seventy degrees. Next, he made a quick survey of the flues, and with the tobacco stick that Uncle Frank had given him Jubal knocked away several leaves that had fallen onto the piping hot flues. In spots nearest the furnace, the flues in a killing barn were cherry red, far too hot to brush leaves away by hand. Loose leaves dropping from poorly looped bundles onto hot flues during killing heats were the direct causes of most barn fires.

Getting out of a killing barn was more of a challenge than getting in. Uncle Frank and Jubal solved that problem with a bit of ingenuity. As soon as Jubal was safely inside, he would select sample leaves and pass them out to Uncle Frank. Then, while Jubal was working inside, Uncle Frank would be laying an old bed mattress over the door frame, extending it outward. Jubal would hand Uncle Frank the lantern and stick. Jubal would yell "Ready." Uncle Frank would respond, "Come on."

Jubal made his famous rolling dive into the open air.

Returning to the shelter, Uncle Frank examined the test leaves carefully by rubbing, smelling and finally crumpling the leaves between his skeleton-like hands. "Dat barn gwine be done curin' befo daybreak. Hit jus' needs just a tad mo heat."

A drainage ditch ran along the property line that divided the farm and the railroad's right of way. In winter, after the volunteer weeds, including poison ivy and poison oak were burned off, one could easily see the tracks from the vantage point of the barns. In spring and summer the foliage created a partial screen.

The burning of the ditch banks took place in the fall, with everyone on the farm pitching in. Much like the U. S. Forestry folks, the farmer would deliberately set fires, and it was their responsibility to control them.

Jubal was tossing wood into the killing furnace, but his attention leaned toward the railroad tracks. As he tossed fresh wood atop the furnace filled with hot coals, sparks flew. Suddenly he noticed what appeared to be headlights of a car or truck shinning in his direction from across the tracks. The boy blinked to clear his eyes. When he opened them, the headlights were gone. "Just my imagination," Jubal thought, "who could be over there at this time on night?"

Just as Uncle Frank and Jubal were finishing their round of the barns the train arrived. The Doppler effect of the staccato puffs of wasting steam grew steadily louder, transmitting the news that the train was coming directly at them. Moments later the sound softened and they knew that the locomotive was bending its way around the town and would soon be opposite the barns. The beam of the locomotive's headlight was soon creating eerie shadows amid the intervening woods as it advanced. When the engine was directly opposite the river barns, less than one hundred yards away, the locomotive stopped. The glow from its open firebox was now helping to illuminate the spot where the iron horse stopped. Jubal knew the routine. He expected the engine to reverse its previous course at any moment. The brakeman got off so he could open the switch to the cars loaded with pulpwood. But minutes passed. Jubal watched the locomotive simply fade away. The bellicose breathing of the iron monster reduced to nothing. Jubal could still see the glow from the firebox in the cab of the locomotive. But something wasn't right. The boy noticed that the locomotive's running lights were barely visible.

Uncle Frank and Jubal began to exchange glances and guesses. Finally they each voiced the same question at the same

24

time, "What in the world is going on over yonder?" Jubal was puzzled, but he was not concerning himself with any potential problems on the engine. He was trying to figure a way that he could snag a ride on the pulpwood engine. He was thinking, "The caboose has been dropped off at the top of town and is more than a mile away and around a deep curve. This means that I don't have to worry about no conductor." The boss of freight trains always worked out of the caboose. The boy knew that the conductor was likely to be the only person who would object to his riding in the locomotive.

At four a.m. Jubal and Uncle Frank were expecting all hands for the pre-breakfast chore of "taking out" or emptying the "aired out" barn. The tobacco, having been declared cured by Frank Ruffin, would be taken to a temporary "packing house" for storage until the curing season was over. That move would make room for today's harvest from the field and restart the curing cycle. Before nightfall the empty barn would be refilled with green tobacco, and the "raising" process would begin again.

With a quick glance at Uncle Frank's clock, the boy knew his father and the others were not due for almost an hour. Jubal was about to say goodbye to Uncle Frank, when he noticed that someone must have closed the firebox door. That glow, too, had disappeared. Uncle Frank noted, " I ain't heahin' nuthin' but bullfrogs and crickets. Whut you hearin' boy?"

"I'm hearin' what you're hearin'."

There were no batteries in steam locomotives in 608's class. Electrical current for the locomotive's running lights was produced by a steam-driven dynamo. When the steam pressure neared zero, so did the direct source and supply of electrical current for 608's running lights. Jubal watched the headlight beam slowly disappear. Then total darkness. It was as if the orchestra had stopped playing and the lights dimmed in his personal theater. The greatest show of the his life was about to begin.

"Whut's happin'?" Uncle Frank echoed the boy's question. Both were convinced now that something was wrong.

"Maybe they're gone," Jubal suggested.

"Nah, dey hain't gone. Locomotives can do a heapa powerful things, but sneakin' off ain't one of dem. Naw, suh, deah's sumthin' wrong over yonder."

"Well, I'm gonna find out."

"You be careful, boy, and don't be gone more'n ten minutes. I'm a' settin' my clock on yo."

Chapter 6: The Railroad Watch

Jubal crossed the open ground in a flash and entered the lightly wooded area in full stride, determined to make the most of his ten minutes. The boy was familiar with the path, and he was totally surprised when he ran smack into a structure that he likened to a sturdy tree. The impact and sudden stop temporarily knocked the breath out of him. Instead of being up a tree, however, Jubal found himself in the grasp of a large man. Scared and hurt, Jubal began desperately to search for air. When breath came, he yelled, "Help! Uncle Frank! Help! There's a man over here and he's trying to kill me!"

"Whut's gwin' on out deah, Jube? Is yo hurt? Keep a' talkin boy, I'z comin."

The man held Jubal in a vise-like grip with one hand. He slapped his other big sweaty hand over the boy's mouth and said, "I'm not going to hurt you, boy. But I've gotta keep you from going over to the train. We're having a problem with the boiler, and if you go over there you could get hurt."

The man moved his sweaty hand and waited for the boy to respond.

"You didn't have to scare me to death. Why didn't you just come over to the barn or just holler at us."

"Listen boy, I ain't got time to argue with you. Promise me you'll get your smart little butt back where you came from and I'll let you go. Deal?"

"Listen, mister, this is my daddy's farm, and I'll go where I want to go. And, you ain't got no right to stop me."

Uncle Frank was very close to them now. Man and boy watched as the boy's mentor frantically stumbled toward them. The old man was wielding a stout tobacco stick, but he was probably more of a menace to himself than anyone else. The big man's body and clothing reeked of sweat and whiskey. The boy was on the verge of throwing up. Had he been thinking clearly, he probably would have done just that--- all over the man holding him. Instead, he began kicking the man's legs wildly with his heels, while the big man held a tight grip on him.

27

"Whar is yo, Jube?" Uncle Frank asked as he approached them in the dark.

The man spoke. "Your boy is right here and he's all right. I stopped him because we're having trouble with the locomotive. It isn't safe for him to go over there until we get it fixed. We did a dumb thing and let the boiler run out of water. As soon as it cools down we're gonna take on fresh water. We don't think anything is gonna happen when we do, but...."

The man's explanation was interrupted by a voice from the direction of the railroad track, "C'mon Lacy, we're gonna give it a try. Let's go."

"OK, Spence, tell George I'll be right there," and to Uncle Frank, he said, "Have we got a deal?"

"Sho we have. I ain't wantin' nobody hurt, much less dis boy. Jus' let de chile go and I'll sees dat he stays wid me over yonder at de barns."

The man released the boy, and without another word was gone. On their way back to the barn the boy said, "What did I tell ya, Uncle Frank?"

"Tell me whut?"

"That this was going to be exciting, that's what! They ain't fooling me, that locomotive ain't about to blow up. Nah, that's a mean bad bunch over there. I'll bet they're all drunk. That big galoot smelled like a drunk skunk."

"Now you listen to me, Jube, and listen real good. Yo ain't gonna go over to no locomotive until me or yo daddy say so, do you heah me?"

"But Uncle Frank," Jubal protested.

"Deh hain't no use boy, I done give de man mah word. And besides, even if'n dey is up to some foolishness, yo sho' nuff ain't got no business over deah."

"But I do have business over there," Jubal insisted.

"What kinda business?"

"I've got th' man's watch, that's what. Here it is right here."

"Lawse me, Jube, whut in de world done possessed yo to steal de man's watch. I'ze ashamed o' yo, Jube."

"I didn't 'xactly steal it. He grabbed me first, didn't he? He didn't have no right to do that. He grabbed me and so I grabbed

28

his ole watch. He's right over there. Let me go over there and give it back to him, please?" Jubal pleaded.

"Dat watch needs to go back to dat man right enough, but we'ze gonna have to figur some other way sizen you goin' over deah. I ain't goin' back on my word. If whut dat man say is true, dey's gonna be down deah fur a long spell. Hit's gone be way yonder late in de mornin' afo' dat biler gwine be cool enuf fo cold water. Dey come up heah red hot and under a full head o' steam. We'll let yo pappy decide about de watch when he gets heah."

Uncle Frank reduced Jubal's chances of returning the watch to zero by taking possession of it. At this point Jubal knew that he was in big, big trouble. "You can't do this to me, Uncle Frank. I didn't mean to take the man's watch, honest I didn't. If Papa finds out I took the man's watch, he's gonna kill me. I know he will. You know that's the truth, don't you?"

"Now, now, quit yo frettin' now, boy, you knows Uncle Frank don't want you to git in no trouble wid yo pappy. We'ze gwine hab plenty o' time and ways to git dat watch back. When we git done heah, I'll take hit ovah to de man myself."

Jubal reacted to Uncle Frank's offer with an idea of his own. "I've got it. I'll just say I found the watch on the ground after the man left. That's it. We'll tell Papa I just found the thing after the man went back to the train."

"Naw, son, we ain't tellin' your Papa no lie. Lies don't never work out in de end. De good Lawd ain't made de world dat way. Yo just give yo ole Uncle Frank some time to think about dis predicament. He's gone take care of this fo you one way or de other. Ain't no need to fret."

Then, as if to change the subject Uncle Frank said, "Dis heah's a mighty fine lookin' timepiece." The old man put the watch against his best ear. "I don't heah no tickin'. Is hit workin'?"

"Let me listen. You couldn't hear it if it was ticking," the frustrated boy responded disrespectfully.

Jubal took the watch and put it to his ear. No sound. The boy read the time by lantern light. 8:15. Jubal gave the watch a violent shake and looked again. The second hand was not moving. He then bumped the watch against the palm of his free hand and looked again."

"No, sir, this watch is just like that locomotive over there; they're both graveyard dead."

"You mussa broke de man's watch."

"I ain't broke his ole watch. Look. It stopped on 8:15. That proves the thing was broke before I took it, don' it?"

"Boy, I sho hope you didn't break dat man's valuable timepiece."

Jubal wanted to say, "Well then, since it's such a valuable piece of property, why don't you let me take it to him." But, the boy knew that the old man's mind was made up.

As they reached the barn shelter, Uncle Frank's alarm went off. That unsettling noise settled the timepiece argument, at least for the near term. The raising barn was three degrees warmer, and the killing heat was holding steady. Uncle Frank also visited the airing barn, where he found the flaccid texture of the leaves to his liking. Then the alarm was reset and another ten-minute break began. The boy was sure that Uncle Frank was as curious as he was to learn what was going on down at the track. The boy knew this because Uncle Frank said the most curious thing.

"Yo know de real reason I can't let yo go over deah, don't yo, boy?

"Sure I do. But, just so I'm real, real sure, why don't you tell me anyway?"

"Naw, you wouldn't believe old Uncle Frank if'n he told yo."

"Try me. I believe the things you tell me about the old days in Fallston."

"Yo does?"

"Sure I do."

"Cause dragons dey always dies at daybreak, dat's why."

The boy could barely keep from laughing out loud, but he knew that laughing at the old man would kill any chance of going to the train. Instead he asked, "Dragons? You mean fire-out-the-nose dragons? Were those things still around when you were a boy? Let me go see, Uncle Frank. Maybe there is a real dragon over there."

"Deh ain't no real dragon over deah, boy. You knows dat good as I does. Spozen' yoh papa comes heah, and I tell him I sent you down deah to looking fur arey dragon? Nah, hit's just dat my old pappy used to tell me stories bout dragons when I was a boy like yo. One of dem stories just sprung in my head, dat's all. I reckon hit's because dat locomotive ovah yonder is the nearest thing to airy real dragon as yoh ole Uncle Frank gwine evah see. I knows you wants to take Mister Lacy's watch yonder to him, but hit's too dangerous. Dat dragon ovah yonder ain't total dead yet. Deah's a heapa fire in dat yonder dragon's belly yet. My pappy told me never to mess around wid no dying dragon."

Chapter 7: The Explosion

The status quo continued. Frank Ruffin was wary of what the boy in his charge might do, so it was no surprise that they were both facing the direction of the locomotive when fireworks suddenly lit up the northern sky. It began as a fireworks display and looked like a volcano erupting in the flatlands. Ashes and red hot cinders spewed high into the air. A deafening boom immediately followed the short pyrotechnics. A powerful whoosh of air forced every leaf and branch in its path to sway and quiver. As the blast wave passed the boy, he saw the boiler rising into the air. It seemed to be in slow motion, turning lazy end-over-end flips. It reminded the boy of a stuffed animal that had been tossed by its tail into the air. It was over within a very few seconds. Then silence.

By lantern light the boy saw the shock on Uncle Frank's face. Jubal never knew which shocked the old man most: the explosion or the boy's statement.

The boy stood on the threshold of the greatest tragedy that he had ever witnessed and calmly predicted, "Well, Uncle Frank, I don't guess old Mr. Lacy will be needing his ole watch now."

At the sound of the explosion, Callie Parsons sprang quickly out of bed and rushed to the window. She saw only a few sparks sifting their way randomly down into the woods near the railroad track. Within seconds Miriam, Miss Parsons' cook and maid was outside her lady's door wanting to know what happened. Callie Parsons did not answer immediately. She was engrossed in watching the car come out of the woods path, turn onto Circle Drive and speed quickly out of town. Miriam was hysterical now. "Are you all right in there, Miss Callie?"

"Yes, yes, Miriam, for heaven sakes I'm fine. Tell Edward to get out and find out what's happened. Tell him to see if the loaded pulpwood cars are all right. And fix us a pot of coffee. I'll be right down." To herself, Callie Parsons said, "If that blast had anything to do with God's answer to my prayer, he sure believes in answering with a bang!"

For a moment the boy thought Uncle Frank was going to send him to the site of the explosion, but the old man ordered him to go home instead. Before Jubal reached his house, he noticed that the lights were already on. The boy's father met him in the yard. Sarah Ruffin, Uncle Frank's wife was there, too.

"It's the train. The pulpwood locomotive blew up right by our barns! I talked to one of the men just before it exploded." The boy's side was aching from the half-mile run. He was panting and talking at the same time.

"Where's Uncle Frank? Is he OK? Are you all right?" Mason Scott was full of questions.

"Yes, sir, we're both all right. One of the railroad men wouldn't let me go down to the train. I guess he saved my life. That man may be dead now. After the explosion, I couldn't hear anything, but Uncle Frank wouldn't let me go down there."

Sarah Ruffin grabbed the boy and wouldn't let him go. She kept repeating, "Thank you, Lawd Jesus."

The elderly couple lived in a small house just behind the big house where the Scotts lived. Aunt Sarah, twenty years younger than her husband, did the housekeeping and cooking for Jubal and his father.

"What man are you talking about, Jube?" The boy's father was probing for any information about the apparently doomed crew.

"His name was Lacy, at least that's what one of the other railroad men called him."

"You saw more than one of them?"

"No, sir, I only saw one, but I heard another man call this man Lacy's name."

Things were happening fast now. Several of the farmhands gathered quickly in the yard. Someone hitched a pair of mules to the big wagon. Mason Scott shared a brief report with them. The farm hands began scrambling onto the wagon. "Brodus, you come with me, " Mason Scott shouted into the crowd, and to Sarah Ruffin said, "Take Jube inside. I'll be right back. I'm going to take a look around down there and I'll send Uncle Frank to the house as soon as I've had a chance to talk to him." Brodus Ruffin was Uncle Frank and Aunt Sarah's son. He was also

34

Scott's main man on the farm. Whenever Mason Scott wasn't around, Brodus was the boss.

The pickup truck carrying Mason Scott and Brodus Ruffin reached the path to the barn before the wagon loaded with excited people got there. The pickup was soon out of sight. Jubal, wanting to be where the action was, was not happy. He considered himself to be a celebrity and wanted to be treated like one. But even more, he wanted to please his father. Jubal wanted his father to stop blaming him for making Mason Scott the loneliest man in the world. Whenever Mason Scott looked at his son, the boy knew. Thankfully, here on the farm the boy was surrounded by people who genuinely cared for him. The blacks, with whom he lived, worked and played gave Jubal far more love and attention than he deserved.

The boy's stress was greatly relieved by the wonderful breakfast Aunt Sarah soon set before him. By the time Uncle Frank and Mason Scott joined Jubal at the kitchen table, Jubal had consumed several pancakes, sausages and a huge glass of fresh milk. Aunt Sarah ran to Uncle Frank and kissed and hugged him. Although the boy had been told that the couple had been married for fifty years, he thought that this was probably their very first embrace. Jubal's father ignored the emotional display, poured coffee for himself and motioned the three to sit.

Mason Scott was thirty-five years old, but he looked older. His wife Belle had been sick from the day the couple's only child Jubal was born, when they lived on a small farm between Martin and Fallston. Jubal's mother died when he was six. She lived six torturous months after a large tumor was removed from her brain.

Mason Scott lost his farm, and he sharecropped for two years after that.

When the overseer's job came open at the old Fallston place last fall, Scott signed on. Here, both father and son were beginning to show signs of recovery. Mason's lean body was still as hard as pig iron, but there had been some softening of his rigid countenance lately. Mason was, as always, a fair man, respected by everyone. During his wife's illness, he'd become a humorless man, not the kind of person people enjoyed being around.

Jubal's father was, as usual, all business that morning.

"What about the men from the train?" the boy asked.

"All three of the locomotive's crew died in the explosion," Mason Scott answered without emotion.

He gave Sarah Ruffin a long look. The boy thought that his father was going to ask her to leave, but if that were the case, he changed his mind. He then turned his gaze, first on Uncle Frank and then onto the boy.

"I want you two to tell me exactly what happened down there this morning. Take your time, and don't leave out anything."

Mason Scott had a stare that pinned the scenery back. Thankfully for both the boy and Uncle Frank, Mason Scott was dividing his gazes between them. "I know there's going to be a big investigation. You two will be asked a lot of questions before this business is over. I want to know what you saw, what you heard and most of all what you did. Which one of you wants to speak first?"

"You go first, Uncle Frank," the boy offered, hoping that Uncle Frank would explain the watch business in a favorable light.

"Naw, son, I 'preciate you thinkin' bout yo ole Uncle Frank, but I believe hits yo dat yo daddy's most interested in hearin' from."

Except for the part about the watch, Jubal told his father every detail that he could remember. He had forgotten about seeing headlights before the train got to the barns. When Jubal finally fell silent, his father asked, "Are you sure you smelled whiskey on the man called Lacy?"

"Yes, sir, he'd been drinkin' all right. He stank so bad it almost made me throw up."

Frank Ruffin then told his story. His report was a mirror image of Jubal's. Not a word about the watch.

"I think this man you ran into," Mason said, "has been in the news before. If I remember correctly, a man named Brandon was one of the crewmen of the switch engine that crushed a man

36

to death last year at the Centerville railroad shops. That happened about this time last year. A pipefitter working under a passenger coach was crushed to death. Supposedly there were warning flags posted to warn the locomotive crew that someone might be working under that coach. I can't remember the name of the man who was killed, but I'm pretty doggone sure this guy Lacy, the man who you say kept you away from the engine, was in charge of the yard engine that day."

Mason Scott paused and rubbed his thin chin with a calloused hand.

"Yes, yes," he continued, "I'm sure. That's the name all right. Lacy Brandon's name was in all the papers back then. I remember now. Most of the shopmen blamed the accident on this guy Brandon. If I remember correctly, Brandon was the head switchman of the yard engine crew that day. The shopmen think that the other men in Brandon's engine crew covered up for him. There was a big investigation, but nothing was ever proven. Apparently the flag that would have gotten Brandon and his crew fired, and maybe a jail sentence to boot was never found. Because of Brandon's involvement in that case, if for no other reason, this explosion is going to make big, big news."

"Uncle Frank, your story is fine. But Jube, I'm worried about this whiskey business." And turning to Frank Ruffin, Mason asked, "Uncle Frank, did you smell whiskey on Mr. Brandon?"

"Naw, suh, I can't rightly say dat I did, but I didn't git nowhere close to de man like Jube wuz. Dat po chile was right in dat man's face."

Turning again to his son, Mason said, "Now, Jube, I'm not saying you're wrong about the whisky, but there is a chance that you could be wrong about that. The man probably had been drinking. But the fact remains that he saved your life. And since he saved your hide, we at least owe him the benefit of the doubt. You see, son, Brandon was on the job at the time of his death. If the railroad gets wind that he had been drinking on the job, it could damage the man's reputation and hurt his family. The presence of alcohol could also have an affect on any insurance settlement in the case. I'm not asking you to lie or even forget about smelling whisky on the man. I'm just telling you that for the time being, let's keep the whiskey business with the people in this room. Is that clear?"

The requested promises were made, and Mason Scott rose to leave. "I'll be around the river barns. You two try to get some sleep. If anyone needs to talk to either of you, I'll bring them along to the house." To his housekeeper Mason Scott ordered, "I'm leaving this pair in your charge, Aunt Sarah. If anyone shows up here wanting to see Uncle Frank or Jube, you send them to the barn; tell them they have to see me first."

Jubal went to the kitchen window and watched his father leave. As soon as he was out of sight, the boy turned to Uncle Frank, "Why in the world didn't you tell Papa about the watch? You promised me you'd take care of it for me, now didn't you?"

"In de fust place it twern't my business to say nuthin' bout no watch, Jube. Weze partners and friends you and me. You took de man's watch and you had yo reasons fo takin' hit. I figured you had yo reasons fur not tellin' yo pappy bout hit too. Deah ain't no way I'm gwine tell sumpthin' bout yo wid out yo permission. Naw, sirree, partners don't do things like dat to one another."

"Well, what am I gonna do? Papa's gonna kill me when he finds out."

"Listen, Jube, deah ain't nobody in dis whole world size me an you knows bout dis watch. Yo pa done said fo us to keep de business of smellin' whiskey wid de people right heah in dis room, aint dat right?"

"Yes sir, that's what he said about me smelling whiskey on the man all right. But what's that got to do with the watch I took off the man?"

"Well, yo' Uncle Frank takes what yo pappy say bout de whiskey to mean dat you pa don't wont dis business to git no mo complicated dan necessary. Like yo pappy say bout de whiskey, we ain't gwine foget bout dat watch neither. But, fer de time bein' let's me and yo keep dat business between us two. How 'bout dat?"

Jubal went for the idea instantly. The boy was soon in bed and fast asleep. Around noon, Aunt Sarah came into Jubal's

38

room and told the boy that dinner was ready and that his father and a dressed-up man were waiting to see him in the dining room.

Chapter 8: Demoted

Frank Ruffin and Jubal told their stories to the reporter, and the newspaper photographer took their pictures. Good. It began to look as if this might be Jubal's day to shine after all. Mason Scott then transported his son back to the river barns. There, however, the boy's status as a living legend came to an instant and humiliating halt. Instead of enjoying an afternoon of being celebrated, Jubal was unceremoniously stuck with the job of handing tobacco. Even worse, his boss for the afternoon was none other than Dove Ruffin, a mere woman.

Dove, the daughter-in-law of Uncle Frank and Aunt Sarah and wife of Brodus, had the reputation of being the best, fastest and most demanding tobacco looper in the county. Dove's three children, all girls, plus the deposed celebrity made up the quartet of Dove's handers.

Handing tobacco was not an ego boost for anybody, especially for a person of Jubal's station and stature. Everybody in North Carolina knew that handing was the lowest of many lows on a tobacco farm, usually performed by children, and mostly girls. Curing, trucking, priming, taking off and hanging were jobs fit for men and boys.

As soon as his father was out of sight, Jubal made sure that he registered his displeasure with everyone at the barn shelter, especially Dove Ruffin. Jubal had become an expert at showing his displeasure.

Dove's workstation consisted of a homemade wooden rack called a looping horse, a ball of heavy cotton thread also known as tobacco twine, and hundreds of tobacco sticks.

Tobacco sticks were rough-cut lumber strips about one-inch square and cut to a uniform length of five feet. The average tobacco barn would hold about six hundred "looped" sticks of green tobacco. This translated into about three hundred sticks per day for each looping station. Sixty bundles of six leaves each could be looped onto each stick, making a total of more that one hundred thousand leaves handed by each crew in a single day. Twenty-five thousand leaves of tobacco handed in a single day is not child's play today.

Tobacco sticks also served another important use. Every tobacco farm boy, and many country girls, owned fine stables of tobacco stick horses. Jubal named his prize stallions Vinegar and Veedeevoo. At that moment his stick pals were stabled in the corner of his room, waiting patiently for their master to come home.

The looping horse served as a rack for the tobacco while bundles from the handers were being "looped" onto them with tobacco twine. Each looper was served by several handers. The hander's job was to make uniform bundles of the loose tobacco leaves that were trucked from the field to the looping station. Each bundle consisted of from three to eight leaves. The number of leaves per bundle depended on the size of the leaves. Ragged, mismatched, uneven, odd-sized, broken or otherwise irregular bundles were summarily rejected and unceremoniously thrown back into the tobacco slide by the looper. Words were not necessary. Accepted bundles were looped. Alternating bundles were flipped across the sticks to serve as counterweights. The quality of the looper's work was crucial to the success of the tobacco harvesting process. Sloppy looping often resulted in disaster. Poorly looped leaves dropping onto red hot flues was the stuff that barn fires were made of.

A second looping crew worked the opposite side of the tobacco truck. Ten people, women and children, performed the job of looping at the barns. An extra person looked after the day curing, hung the looped sticks in temporary racks, and performed other chores as needed. The four primers in the field plus the trucker who shuttled the carts back and forth from the field added to a total of sixteen people who worked from before dawn to dark on this one small farm.

The boy was anxious to go over and view the aftermath of the explosion. He had a plan: do such sloppy, sorry work that Dove would beg him to leave. The few bundles he handed were rejected. To the extent that Dove was getting upset with him, the boy's plan was working. He knew that Dove would keep her mouth shut and never complain to his father. Instead of releasing Jubal, Dove Ruffin, who was reading the boy's mind right down to the small print, suggested a plan of her own.

"Look, Jube, why don't you git yoself straight and help us catch up? Then you'll have time to run over yonder."

"What'a you mean? I'm working as hard as I can. Can't you see that?"

"Oh, you're working hard all right. Nobody can do as sorry as you're doing by no accident."

Jubal assessed their situation. Dove was right. With a little hustle the barn crew could catch up. The day was another scorcher, and the field was much hotter than the shade of the barn shelter where the looping was being done. Furthermore, the smaller top leaves now being cropped in the field meant that it was taking longer for the croppers to fill a truck. The boy peered into the near-empty truck. Then he looked in the direction where the next mule-powered tobacco slide would come. Nothing in sight. The boy did a complete reversal and began handing two bundles to each one the girls handed.

Dove's plan worked. Instead of dragging, Jubal became the motivator. With eight handers and the two loopers hustling, the truck was quickly emptied. Only a minute later, Jubal was looking at what was left of engine 608. The main part of the locomotive remained on the track. Huge pipes and sheets of boilerplate from the frame of the engine were pointing skyward, as if the base and outstretched pipes were waiting for the boiler to fall back into its cradle. The boiler, however, was showing no signs of coming back. It lay half buried in the track-side ditch about 100 feet ahead. The engine tender and the rest of the pulpwood train were nowhere in sight. People were everywhere. The current crop of curiosity seekers were strangers to Jubal. Most of the town folk had been there much earlier. Entrance to the cab of the engine had been chained and locked. Curtains at the windows had been lowered. "No Trespassing" signs had been posted on all sides of the motionless locomotive frame.

Jubal was staring at the window, when he heard a man's voice. "The bodies have all been taken away, if that's what you're wondering, son."

"Then why won't they let us see in there?"

"Believe me, son, you don't really want to see in there," the man answered.

"Do you work for the railroad?" Jubal asked.

"Yes."

"When are you going to take the engine away?"

"I'm not sure, son. Right now we're still trying to find out exactly what happened."

"Well, shucks, I can tell you that. They put cold water in a red hot boiler, and the thing just blew up. I saw the boiler go a mile in the air myself."

"So you're the kid who talked to Brandon just before the explosion?"

Jubal had just enough time to say, "Yes, sir," before Robin Ruffin interrupted.

"Mama says for you to come on right now, Jube. We got another truck to loop. She said to tell you Boots ain't goin back to de field neither."

Jubal would have ignored Robin's first sentence. But the second grabbed his attention. Those words meant that his father could be at the barn any minute. His father and the other men would always bring in the last truck. That could happen anytime.

"I've got to go now," the boy told the red-faced railroad detective.

"You know, kid, what's the strangest thing about the explosion?"

"No, sir, but I really have to go now." The boy was listening more for sounds from the barn now than from the man. The man was talking more to himself than to Jubal, but the boy clearly understood the man to say, "All three of those men's watches were still working! Isn't that amazing? By the way son, I'll need to--" The man's voice trailed off as he noticed the boy was now completely out of hearing, and it wasn't good for a railroad detective to be caught talking to himself.

Jubal's situation had taken a dangerous turn. Now he was really in trouble. He desperately needed to talk with Uncle Frank. From what the railroad man just said, Jubal was even more convinced that the man who grabbed him was not one of the locomotive crew. The boy passed Robin along the way without slowing or speaking and was back at his looping station before the girl came in sight.

"Did you see Robin?" But before the panting boy could catch enough breath to answer, Dove continued: "I don't know 'bout Robin, but you musta seen the devil. Are you all right? You look awful. Go lay down on your cot over yonder. I see your daddy coming. He'll get somebody to take you on up to the house."

Everyone on the farm knew that Jubal was subject to sudden and violent headaches. They all knew that the only known treatment was to leave the boy alone. The course of Jubal's headaches was predictable: vomit, heave, hibernate in a dark place, and sleep-- in that order.

"You didn't have no business over where that mess is, but you had to go. And now you done went," Dove criticized.

Mason Scott and the other three primers from the field arrived at the barns within minutes. With extra hands the full crew made short work of the looping.

Soon it was time to hang tobacco. Normally, this was the happiest and most romantic part of the tobacco harvester's day. The four men, including Jubal's father would scramble high overhead, up into the barn rafters. Jubal long envied these men and dreamed of the time when his legs would stretch from rafter to rafter. Then he'd really be respected.

It turned out that Jubal was not sick, merely winded from his frantic run from the trackside to his workstation. The boy proudly took his spot in the receiving and passing chain. This bucket-brigade type operation would stretch, person to person, from the temporary racks outside the barns to a spot below the lowest man in the rafters. From there it was up to the men in the rafters to distribute the sticks evenly from top to bottom and side to side in order to maximize every inch of available curing space.

At least Jubal was qualified for this line of work. The younger children or those not strong enough to properly handle the heavy sticks of green tobacco were excluded from this process and released to run and play.

It was not unusual for a song to break out as the rafters were being filled. But the boy was so engrossed in his own troubles that he was completely surprised to hear Brodus' deep bass lead.

"Swing low sweet chariot, coming for to carry me home.

I looked over Jordan and what did I see?

A band of angels comin after me,

Coming for to carry me home."

The boy was not in the mood for singing. But he did want the angels to come and carry him home--carry him to a home where he would be loved and forgiven of his sins.

Chapter 9: Promoted

Jubal rode home on the wagon with the barn hands that evening. The mule-drawn conveyance served as a local farm bus. The wagon made stops to drop off the women and children at the tenant houses scattered along the way. As expected, Uncle Frank was at the mule barn when the wagon arrived there. When not curing tobacco, the barn was Uncle Frank's assigned duty station. His job was mostly ceremonial. If he had a written job description, it probably would have read, "look after" the livestock. Uncle Frank saw to it that all the farm animals were healthy, fed, watered and cared for. Frank Ruffin was always doing something. Whether as veterinary consultant, weather expert or simply as a storyteller, Frank Ruffin's presence was considered essential to the well-being of the place.

The other men on the farm did the barnyard tasks that required manual labor, such as filling troughs with water, tossing hay into the overhead feeding racks and removing the stable manure.

Sarah Ruffin, who was spry in her seventies, usually fed the chickens, milked the cow and carried slops to the hogs.

Brodus, Boots and Thad unhitched the mules and turned them into the dirt floored lot. The huge animals demonstrated that they were glad to be home by rolling in the thick dust and kicking their heels in the air upside down. The old man kept a supply of homemade lye soap at the barn, and the four males, including Jubal, took turns pumping water and washing tobacco gum from their hands. Comparatively, the tobacco gum was not nearly as heavy as it was earlier in the season, and the men made short work of the cleanup. When the season began, and the bottom leaves called lugs were being primed and cured, the gum was extremely heavy and hard to get rid of.

The boy was hoping that the other men would leave quickly so that he could have a private talk with Uncle Frank. But the men were in no hurry to leave. Everybody had lots to talk about that day.

Jubal could see his father talking to the red-faced railroad detective some distance away near the farmhouse. The man had been waiting at the house to talk with his father. Jubal watched the detective and his father from inside the barn. There were a number of knot holes available and this trick was not new to the boy. After a few minutes, the detective left. Mason looked toward the barn, obviously looking for Jubal.

Finally, the other men left the stable area and the boy's father went into the house. Jubal told Uncle Frank what the detective said about the dead men's watches.

"Dis heah watch business is getting mo' worrisome all de time," Uncle Frank muttered mostly to himself.

"Do you think Mr. Brandon had two watches?"

"Hit's possible."

"Possible? That's just great. I know it's possible. But who can this second Mr. Brandon possibly be? That's what I want to know."

"I heah whut yo sayin', boy. If'n either one of dem Mr. Brandons happens to still be 'live, den we sho 'nuff done got ourselfs sumthin' wuth worrin' 'bout ."

"Oh me, Uncle Frank, I just remembered something else, too."

"Whut's dat?"

"Just before the train got to the barns, I was throwing wood in the killing barn furnace. I saw car or truck lights shining towards the tracks from the town side. This second Mr. Brandon coulda' been in that car that come up over by the tracks just before the locomotive got there."

"How come you ain't said nuthin' bout dis befoh, Jube?"

"I guess I just forgot. I wasn't sure. I'm still not sure. I coulda' just been seeing spots from looking into the fire."

"Listen, Jube, yo 'magination's is bout to land you and me both in a heap o' trouble."

"I can't help that now. That watch I took off that man ain't no imaginary watch. Anyhow, what's done is done. It's what's going to happen next that's worrying me now. What do you really think? Do you really believe there was two Mr. Brandons?"

48

"What I think don't make no difference. But hits de truth dat's whut counts a whole heap. You gotta stop dis frettin' over dat watch and all dis stuff bout two Mr. Brandons. Just think 'bout hit dis way. If dat watch belong to Mr. Brandon, he ain't in no hurry to get it back. You done said that yoself, ain't' dat right?"

"Yes, sir."

"Now spossen dat watch do belong to somebody else. Somebody dat's just pretendin' to be Mr. Brandon, den whut?"

"I don't know, Uncle Frank. I tell you I just don't know. That's exactly the thing I'm worried about."

"You 'member whut I said about deah bein' a dragon a'dyin' down by de track dis mornin'?"

"Yes, sir. But, afterwards you said there really ain't no such thing as a dragon. I guess that meant that you were just pretending. You knew all along that there wasn't any dragon down there."

"Dat's 'xactly right. And later on dat's 'xactly whut I said. Hit wuz jus' one ole man's 'magination whut got de best of him fer a little spell, dat's all dat wuz."

"OK, so now I understand what you meant about the dragon. But, what's that got to do with this Mr. Brandon's watch?"

"I'm a sayin' dat if you starts a talkin' bout two Mr. Brandons, you gwine sound a heap mo peculiar dan Uncle Frank a talkin' 'bout dat dragon dying down deah at dem railroad tracks."

"Yes sir, I see what you mean about that all right."

"Who gwine believe you? Everybody says you got too much 'magination now. You ain't doin' nuthin' but bring misery on yosef wid all dis worrin'."

Just then, Aunt Sarah came in the yard and called Jubal to supper. Uncle Frank said, "You run along now and eat yo supper, and just leave de worrin to yo ole Uncle Frank."

Uncle Frank's lecture, as usual, worked wonders. Uncle Frank's spiritual lift, however, was not destined to last very long. As the boy opened the screen door to the kitchen, he saw the sheriff's car turning into his yard. The sheriff was a regular at the boy's house, and ordinarily Jubal would have been glad to see him. But fears of what his father might do to him when and if he finds out about the stolen watch were compounded by the sight of the lawman. Chill bumps ran up the boy's spine and merged with the headache that was beginning to make its way down.

Jubal called into the house, "Papa, Aunt Sarah, Sheriff Bob's here."

Bob Dunbar and Mason Scott had been good friends since boyhood. The elder Scott's mood usually perked up a notch whenever the sheriff came around. Mason greeted his friend with, "Smelled Aunt Sarah's biscuits, eh?"

The sheriff appeared not to be listening. Instead, the rotund lawman made a beeline for the kitchen stove where Aunt Sarah was guiding biscuits onto a plate from a baking tin. It was very hot in the kitchen, but the sheriff gave Aunt Sarah a big hug anyway.

"You best save all dat butterin' up fo yo biscuits," Aunt Sarah said to the overweight lawman.

"Bless your heart, Aunt Sarah. That's mighty good advice."

Soon the three were feasting on fried chicken, butter beans, black-eyed peas, corn on the cob, candied yams, biscuits, butter and homemade grape preserves. The conversation centered, of course, on the explosion and all the attention it was generating in Fallston. Finally the sheriff announced the purpose for his visit. "I just got a call from the funeral director over in Centerville. Mrs. Brandon has requested that Jubal and Uncle Frank come to her husband's funeral this Saturday. He also said there'd be a meal afterward at the church and it would be good if they could stay for that."

And, to Jubal the sheriff said, "I hear your picture is going to be in the paper tomorrow, young man. You're quite a celebrity. Do you'all get the Raleigh paper?" The News and Observer was published in the state capital, Raleigh. It was by far the largest newspaper in the eastern half of North Carolina.

Jubal shook his head.   The sheriff said, "OK, I'll have someone run you out a copy in the morning."

Then turning to Mason he asked, "What can I tell the funeral director? If you can't make it, Mason, I can see that Uncle Frank and Jube get there."

"I don't see why I can't make it. We've got only one more barn to put in and then just a little bit of curing to finish up."

"OK, then it's all set. The funeral's at Mill Creek Baptist Church on Saturday morning at 11 a. m. Do you know where that is?"

"Yep," Mason Scott answered.

Into the kitchen the sheriff yelled, "You're a beautiful woman, Aunt Sarah. Too bad you're already married."

"Go on 'way from heah wid yo foolishness, sheriff. By de look of you, you done told dat to 'bout every cook in dis heah county."

After the sheriff left, Jubal went down to the barn to call Uncle Frank to supper and tell him the news about their pictures in tomorrow's News and Observer. Jubal also told Uncle Frank about their invitation to Lacy Brandon's funeral on Saturday. It was not unusual for blacks to attend funerals at all-white churches. The same thing applied to whites attending black funerals.

"Dat po woman must be aggrievin' somethin' awful."

"Wonder why she wants us to come to his funeral?"

"Cause weze de last people whut's alive dat talked wid her husband, dat's why."

"And she thinks that her husband saved my life?"

"Dat, too. Her husband must'a been a mighty fine man."

"He didn't seem so mighty fine to me."

"Listen, Jube, you gotta git dis kinda thinkin' outta your head. De man wuz in a heapa trouble, time was runnin out, and he didn't have no time to waste on bein' all nice and sweet to you and me. One thing he had on his mind wuz keepin' you from gettin' hurt. And dat's whut he done. Now ain't dat right?"

"Yes, sir, I guess so. Yes, sir, that's what he did all right."

When the boy reached his house, his father greeted him with the news that he'd be trucking tomorrow. James Taylor had been called to the bedside of his ailing father in Richmond. Boots would take James' place in the field. That left Jubal to do the trucking. The boy was told this in his father's usual matter-of-fact manner. His tone of voice was all business. It wouldn't be dark for another couple of hours, but Mason Scott told the boy, "You've had a long night and a longer day. You'd better get some sleep, son. You've got another big day ahead of you tomorrow."

The boy thought, "What kind of day do you think I've had today, Pop?" Suddenly, Jubal realized that his father had just called him son." And, even better, he had given his son the most responsible job of his entire life. To Jubal, trucking tobacco was about the greatest job in the whole world. Trucking was even more prestigious than curing with Uncle Frank. On the curing job, Jubal was only a helper. As the trucker, Jubal Early Scott would be totally, solely and completely in charge of the farm's most valuable commodity all the way from the fields to the curing barns. Today the boy had apparently watched three men die. But now, Jubal Scott wasn't thinking of them. Jubal Early Scott was thinking of his own life, a life that may be beginning at last.

Chapter 10: A Lesson in Journalism

At four a.m. the following day, all hands arrived at the river barns and removed the "killed" tobacco from the barn to make room for that day's harvest. After the tobacco in that barn was packed away in a storage house near the Scotts' farmhouse, everyone except Thad Walker went home for breakfast. Thad was taking the Ninety and Nine Crew's place curing at the river barns. Thad's wife would bring her husband's breakfast when she came to start her day at the looping horse.

After breakfast Boots and Jubal rode Maude and Cindy, the trucking mules, back to the river barns. Jubal's first challenge as a trucker was to harness Cindy to one of the tobacco trucks. Jubal had been around while this job was performed many times. He'd even thought to himself, "I can do this with my eyes shut." But he soon discovered that seeing, thinking and doing are not the same things. Thad Walker offered to give the novice trucker a hand with the hitching chore, but Jubal dismissed him with a shake of his head.   So Thad appeared to busy himself by restacking barn wood in a woodpile nearby where he could keep an eye on the action. Cindy was a gentle, good-natured animal. Up to this point her behavior had been quite predictable. However, one misstep and the boy could be seriously hurt. Cindy, meanwhile was looking on with her big black, all-knowing eyes. She appeared to smile as Jubal tried to raise his nine-year-old voice to nineteen.

By the time Cindy had been backed into the shaft, the harness and most of the chains and rein were either under the mule's feet or on the wrong side. Undaunted, Jubal clipped right hooks into left traces, missed reins loops and generally made a complete mess of the job. Meanwhile, Boots, an old hand at the chore, made short work of hitching Maude. The boy left for the tobacco patch looking very much like a Roman soldier standing tall and proud inside his fertilizer sack chariot. Boots was glowingly proud of being the newest primer on the tobacco farm. In a few minutes he would be snapping the tobacco leaves from their stalks, throwing them into the slide. And, he would be telling Maude when to 'move up' and when to 'whoa' like the other men on the farm.

Jubal called, "Hey Thad, I'm sure I've got everything hooked up right, but how 'bout checking it for me just to make sure. I want to run over and take a look at what's left of that locomotive before I have to leave for the field."

"Sure Jube, you run along over there. Just remember, you need to be leaving for the field in about fifteen or twenty minutes. I'll get everything checked out and have Cindy ready to go when you get back."

Jubal quickly reached the spot where the man had blocked his way and held him captive. He stopped. Jubal wanted to make sure that the big man was not down there waiting for him. No one in sight. But as Jubal made his next step, a big man stepped from behind the dead locomotive cab. Luckily for Jubal, the man's eyes were glued to the ground. The stranger was knocking dirt, rocks and debris around with a stick. The sight sent chills through Jubal's body. He knew what the man was looking for. The boy blinked hard, hoping the man would disappear like the headlights of the phantom car on the night of the explosion. But the man, a big man like the man who grabbed him the night before, was still there.

Seconds later the boy had Cindy in a full trot, and headed in the general direction of the tobacco patch. But Jubal Scott did not resemble a Roman soldier. His entire body was well below the fertilizer skirts of his tobacco truck, considerably lower than Cindy's broad rump. Luckily, Cindy knew the way to the tobacco patch.

When Jubal reached the field, the primers in the patch had made only two ups and downs. The boy's heart was still pounding very fast, but here in the field among his heroes, his fears were rapidly dissipating. When the men and Boots reached the spot where Jubal waited, Jubal's father made an X with the toe of his shoe indicating the row he wanted Jubal's truck to be in after the men completed their next up and down.

Each primer worked two rows, so when the octo-primers went up and down once, altogether they had worked sixteen rows. When the primers returned, Jubal would leave Cindy and his truck for them. Then he and Maude would head for the barn with the partially loaded truck so that the looping could begin. Jubal soon had Cindy squared and properly started in the row indicated by his father. But, to his horror, the boy discovered that he had broken down more than a dozen stalks of tobacco in the process. Manually, Jubal tried to stand the broken stalks upright, only to have them flop over again and again.

Just at the height of his frustration, the truth of his current dilemma became a laughing matter. "I see now why Papa promoted me and Boots at the same time. That's it. Papa knew I'd knock down a whole bunch of stalks before I learned how to get my mule and truck straight in the rows. And, Papa knows that Boots doesn't know exactly which leaves are ripe enough to pick. So what. After today ain't no reason for the stalks to be standing. And, there ain't gonna be no leaves left in the field neither. They're stripping every leaf as they go. There ain't no way that either one of us can mess up."

Jubal began stripping the leaves from the stalks he had knocked down. By the time the primers returned, the boy had covered the bottom of his tobacco slide with the leaves from all his broken plants. Mason Scott looked at the broken stalks, and noticed that the leaves had been cropped, saved and laid neatly in the floor of the truck. Seeing that his son had acted wisely he said, "Both you boys are doing a great job." Boots and Jubal exchanged smiles, and the specter of the man poking around the dead locomotive seemed a thousand miles away.

Before Jubal reached the barns he spotted the rear end of a sheriff's' car, and assumed that the morning paper had arrived. He soon noticed that all the barn hands were huddled around Dove Ruffin. Before the boy could bring Maude to a stop, the mule's head was in the middle of the crowd. Not one of the dozen gathered around Dove even noticed that a thousand-pound, slobbering, snorting mule had joined them. No one noticed Jubal Scott either. To get a glimpse of the paper, Jubal had to climb on top of the table. He read, "TROUBLED TRAIN CREW DIE IN FREAK ACCIDENT."

Dove read:

"The last act of the ill-fated crewmen was a humanitarian one.

Brakeman Lacy Brandon was making his way to a nearby tobacco barn, apparently intending to warn anyone who might be at that barn, when he met nine-year-old Jubal Scott (pictured below). Young Scott, son of the farm's overseer Mason Scott, was spending the night at the barn with Frank Ruffin, who was looking after the curing."

"I wasn't just spending the night at the barn. I was working," Jubal shouted angrily. "Who does that guy think I am?"

Dove stopped reading, and along with all the others, stared at Jubal. They knew he was there now. "Why don't you just sit down over yonder and cool yourself, Jube, and just let me finish what the paper man says before you get yourself all upset. You can have the whole paper in a minute."

Meanwhile, one of the men who had watched Callie Parsons' limo on the morning of August 9, was also reading about the explosion in the Centerville Star. The man's interest was focused on one particularly worrisome line in the local newspaper account, ".......young Jubal Scott, the boy whose life was saved by Lacy Brandon, will be in attendance at Lacy Brandon's funeral on Saturday..."

Callie Parsons was also reading her copy of the News and Observer. She, too, was interested in the fact that Jubal Scott would be attending the funeral. Jubal was about to become a member of her Sunday school class at Fallston Baptist Church. Callie Parsons was also interested in the comments made during the Star's interview with the widow of Lacy Brandon. "--------- the bereaved widow makes no secret of the fact that she believes that her late husband, and the other men in his crew, were murdered. The basis for Mrs. Brandon's claim stems from the verbal attacks, threats and violence which she claims have continuously been made against her husband and this crew for more than a year. Mrs. Brandon is referring to the fatal accident now more than a year ago which claimed...."

By the time the News and Observer was handed to Jubal, he had cooled down considerably. But as he read about Lacy Brandon saving the boy's life, Jubal became upset again with the reporter. After reading the article Jubal concluded that there was no way that Lacy Brandon and the man who grabbed him were one and the same. Moments later, as he studied the photos of the three dead crewmen, Jubal was even more convinced that the man who grabbed him was not among them.

Chapter 11: The Funeral

Because of the Saturday funeral, Friday became a typical Saturday for the Scotts.   After baths in the big wash tub with water from the kitchen stove reservoir, the two went to town. Their first stop was the barber shop in Fallston, where both had haircuts.   There were at least six men ahead of them when they entered the shop, but the Scotts didn't have to wait.   The customers were waiting for their hair to grow. The shop had five chairs but only one barber.   The excess chairs are reminders of Fallston's flourishing old days.   Andy, the barber, and the idlers were talking politics and swapping lies when the Scotts entered the shop.   However, following a short exchange of "Howdy's", only the sound of the clippers could soon be heard. The silence was not unpredictable. Not only was Jubal's father a silent man; he generated an aura of silence wherever he went.

The pair then drove twenty miles to Martin, the county seat. Except for court days and Saturdays, Martin was usually as dead as Fallston. However, unlike Fallston, business would pick up in Martin when the tobacco markets opened and money began to circulate.   Now with no money to circulate, Main Street was all but deserted.   Unless one has experienced a small eastern Carolina town on a dead day, one simply cannot know how dead dead can be. As the pair approached the front door of Legget's Department Store, however, the doors opened as if by magic. This was long before the seeing-eye electric models, but two customer-starved clerks can be just as effective. Jubal's father pointed wordlessly to his son, and the two were immediately ushered into the boys' department. Once there, Mason issued terse and economically sufficient orders.

"Something, not too expensive, that the boy can wear to church---- suit, shirt, tie, shoes and socks." This was sweet music to the eager clerks, and Jubal was treated like royalty.

"Terrible thing about the train explosion over at Fallston," one of the clerks said to Jubal's father.

"Yep," Mason Scott answered. Anybody can say "yep," but, the way Mason Scott said it, it had the effect of closing the subject immediately.

The entire visit to Legget's was all business. Before they left the store, Mason also purchased a shirt, tie and a new suit for himself. While the two waited for alterations, the Scotts treated themselves to a movie and popcorn. They saw the same cowboy movie they would have seen the next day. There were less than a dozen people in the theater. Flash Gordon was soaring along in outer space when they entered. This meant that the Scotts would experience the rare pleasure of seeing the main cowboy movie from the beginning.

While the reels were being changed, Mason told his son that Uncle Frank had decided not to attend the funeral. This news sent questions through Jubal's mind and answers he wasn't going to get from his father. So the boy settled down and enjoyed the movie. Between the action scenes, Jubal's mind kept drifting back to the implications of Uncle Frank not going to the funeral. The more he thought about it, the better he liked the idea. He loved Uncle Frank, but he was envious of the attention Uncle Frank got whenever they were together. Uncle Frank was the most colorful person the boy had known. There was something about Uncle Frank that made people want to listen to what he had to say. Now with Uncle Frank out of the picture, Jubal would get all the attention. The boy knew that his father wasn't going to steal anybody's show.

The road to the Mill Creek church paralleled the railroad tracks which connected Fallston with the rail hub at Centerville. Because of the flatness of the terrain, there were very few curves. The Scotts passed baseball games in progress. White teams were playing against white teams and the black teams were playing against black teams.

As Mill Creek Baptist Church came into view, Mason could see that parking would be a problem. A string of cars had already been parked on the road. Jubal's father followed suit, and the two walked the equivalent of about two city blocks. The number of people milling around in the church yard indicated that the sanctuary was already filled to overflowing. As they

60

moved toward the front door a black-suited man obviously from the funeral parlor, approached them.

"You are Mr. Scott, aren't you?" he asked in a whisper so low that you'd think he was on a putting green. The man's approach suited Jubal's father perfectly. Mason nodded in reply.

"And this must be Jubal?" the man asked softly, patting the boy's new haircut. Mason Scott responded with another nod.

"I take it that Mr. Ruffin will not be attending the funeral. Is that correct?" Mason Scott gave his longest speech of the day. "That's right, Mr. Ruffin wanted to come, but the old fellah was just not up to it." The man nodded politely in response without saying a word.

Mason Scott and this guy were really hitting it off.

"Where are you parked, Mr. Scott?"

Mason pointed.

"You will be going to the grave site?" the man asked, as if "no" would break his heart.

Mason had promised Jubal earlier that they would be going into Centerville directly from the church, and promised that they would be eating at Cameron's Barbecue. Jubal's stomach took a turn for the worse when his father nodded in the affirmative. This man had turned Jubal's father into a mute puppet.

The man raised his voice several octaves when he next spoke. He was clearly pleased and excited now. "Why don't you bring your car here, Mr. Scott," the man said pointing to an imaginary spot on the ground. "Jubal can stay here with me while you do that. We'll wait for you right here. When you get back, I'll get you parked with the family cars. We also have seats reserved in the church for you and your son. I'll seat you as soon as you've parked."

From that moment on, the Scotts' situation went downhill. Five minutes later they were jammed into the third pew from the front, listening to "Rock of Ages" being dolefully played by a lady who could pass for Whistler's mother. As they were being seated all heads turned in their direction. They were a marked pair.

Up front below the pulpit Lacy Brandon's casket was completely covered with alternating arrangements of red roses and white roses. Bouquets of flowers of all varieties extended across the width of the sanctuary. Black clothing, white handkerchiefs and pasteboard fans seemed to be the uniform of the day. People were everywhere. By the time the service began, even the center aisle was not passable. It was so hot that Jubal wondered what kept the flowers from wilting. The interior of the sanctuary felt like the inside of a killing barn.

Suddenly Jubal's attention was shifted from the flowers and the heat. The pastor was speaking, "Knowing Lacy Brandon as we knew him, we are not surprised that the very last thing our dear brother Lacy did on this earth was to save the life of another. There is a lad," turning his head in the Scotts' direction, "here in this service today who owes his very life to Lacy Brandon." That message sent a thousand eyes in the Scotts' direction. People all over the church did the unthinkable and stood to get a peek at the them. Jubal felt a different kind of heat now. He glanced at his father whose face had turned to stone.

From the tracks directly behind the grieving congregation, came a mournful sound of a steam locomotive whistle. Those moments were the equivalent of a fly-over by today's Blue Angels. The pastor had no choice but to pause and grant the lonely whistle its minute. Jubal was certain that the temperature in that place had soared well over one hundred twenty degrees. For one full minute, as the whistle continued to send its plaintive message through that old country church, chill bumps were easily outnumbering drops of sweat.

People patted and hugged the boy and told him how lucky he was a hundred times before he and his father could reach the relative seclusion and safety of the truck cab. Uniformed police cars blocked the eastbound direction when they left the church parking lot, preventing Mason Scott from leaving the procession at the starting point. But as they entered the city, Jubal's father took the first right turn open to him, and he never looked back. If Mason Scott had bothered to look back, he might have noticed that another car made that same exit from the stream of cars with headlights on. The vehicle followed the Scotts' pickup until it was well on its way to Fallston.

Chapter 12: The Tear Drop

The Scotts were back on the farm by one p.m. "Don't fix me anything to eat, Aunt Sarah. I'll pick up something later in Martin," Mason Scott barked in Aunt Sarah's direction as he entered the house. Minutes later Mason was out of his funeral clothes, redressed and gone. Aunt Sarah transferred her attention to Jubal.

"You run upstairs now and change yo' clothes, honey. Aunt Sarah'll have you a plate fixed when you get back down heah."

The old couple had not expected the Scotts to be back from the funeral for several hours. They could see that Mason Scott was upset. Frank and Sarah were anxious to hear all about the funeral, and Jubal was equally anxious to talk. But it was well past his eating time, and he was hungry. Frank paced, and Sarah hovered around above her charge, making sure that his meal went as quickly as possible. Jubal finally downed the last of his milk and started talking. He began with his father's encounter with the man from the funeral home. Nods, "yes, Lawds'" and groans emanated from Sarah. When Jubal came to the part about everyone in the church looking at them, Aunt Sarah injected, "I know dat done tore yo pappy to pieces."

"Couse hit did, but dat preacher won't meanin' no harm apointin' yo out de way he did. He jus' don't know dat Mr. Mason is de way he is," Uncle Frank added.

"Couse he won't meanin' no harm, hits jus a shame Mr. Mason is de way he is," Aunt Sarah concurred.

"You say deah wus lotsa folks deah?" Uncle Frank asked.

"A million at the very least."

Jubal wanted to talk, not answer questions. "Listen, why don't you folks just listen and let me talk. When I get through talking you can ask all the questions, groan, amen, and yes, Lawdy all you want to."

As soon as those angry words left the boy's mouth, a tear ran down Sarah's withered cheek. Hot tears immediately began streaming down the boy's face, too. The boy never imagined that a single tear could carry so much information, a message that

Jubal Early Scott would never forget. Within seconds, Aunt Sarah and Jubal were bawling like babies. Aunt Sarah took the boy into her lap and rocked him for several minutes. Jubal Scott never talked crossly to Aunt Sarah again.

The tearful interlude upset Uncle Frank. "I wish you two would stop all dis blubberin', so I can find out what went on at dat funeral."

"Go on Jube, honey. Aunt Sarah gwine be quiet. Me and your Uncle Frank wants to heah what happened at de funeral."

The boy blew his nose in his funeral handkerchief and continued. The words that now flowed from that nine-year-old were far too mature to suit his age, education or upbringing. Rather, his report was a testimony to what can be learned and absorbed under extraordinary conditions.

"There wasn't a person in the place, except maybe Papa and the preacher that won't crying. I never saw so much crying in my life. The preacher talked on and on about how Mr. Brandon was such a faithful deacon for his Lord, what a true friend he was, what a Christian gentleman and I don't remember what all he said Mr. Brandon was. He said that Mr. Brandon loved everybody, and everyone who really knew him loved him, too. But just like our savior Jesus Christ, this good man was despised, misunderstood, mistreated, hated and rejected by many of his own kind. Throughout this last hectic year of his life, the preacher said, Lacy Brandon took all the hatred heaped upon him just the way Jesus would, even down to the very last act of his life, with gentleness, love, kindness and compassion and doing good for others."

Jubal paused to blow his nose. Aunt Sarah was crying again. Jubal continued. "While the preacher's saying these good things about the man, I'm sitting there thinking about the terrible time I'd spent with him. And the more the preacher talked and the more people cried, the more I knew that either me, or the preacher and all the rest of those people, had to be crazy. Every person in that church acted like they believed every word that the preacher said. And if they're right, I must be crazy."

"I'm telling you, Uncle Frank and Aunt Sarah, the man who grabbed me was not a good man. I might be little and I might be mixed up about a whole lot of things. But I know what I know. I know that man who grabbed me was drunk. Do you believe me? Or do you people think I'm crazy, too? There must be something really bad wrong with me. I'm telling you two, and I'm gonna keep on telling you, there has to be two Lacy Brandons. One Mr. Brandon grabbed me. The other Mr. Brandon is the man the preacher talked about."

The boy began to cry again, and Aunt Sarah held him. Uncle Frank said, "Listen to me, Jube. You ain't de only one who thinks Mr. Brandon was a bad man. A whole heapa folks thinks de man was terrible bad. A whole heapa folks say Mr. Brandon killed somebody and den won't man enough to own up to it. It ain't yo fault dat you feels de way you does 'bout him. Hits' like Lawd Jesus say bout de truth. Jesus say de truth hits like a sword. And, wherever de truth falls, some folks falls on one side and some folks falls on the other side. From what I heah de truth ain't been full knowed bout dat man getting killed under dat train. De truth ain't gone be knowed till de truth bout dat flag is knowed. Everybody got to make up deah own mind which side dey believes de truth is on. Yo is a' sittin' on de edge of dat sharp sword o' truth right now. And dat thing is a' cutting yo to pieces. Come on, boy, let's go see if we can't catch some fish for our supper."

Chapter 13: The Letter

As Melinda Brandon was opening her front door, she noticed that Wally Meecham, the Brandons' regular postman was entering her front gate. "Hi, Wally," she called. "Would you believe that I'm just now on my way to the post office to mail you a letter?"

"Wait right there, ma'am, I've got a bunch of mail for you, too," the mail carrier returned cheerfully. Seconds later on Melinda's front porch the delivery man was handing a batch of letters to the widow Brandon. Similarly, the widow Brandon was poking a packet of letters toward the mailman. Both laughed.

"Look at this. People, most people that is, have been very kind and gracious to me. Lately, I have to spend half my time reading my mail and the other half writing thank-you notes. But I don't mind; people have been wonderful. I can never repay everyone for what they have done and are doing for me. I didn't know there were so many wonderful people in Centerville. Thank you for bringing it all to me, Wally."

"You're very welcome. Here, let me have those. I'll save you a trip to the post office."

"There's really no need; I'm going right by there anyway," Melinda said, "You don't need to carry this extra bundle around all morning. But I do believe there is a note in this batch addressed to you. Just a minute. I can deliver that to you in person if you like."

"No, no, don't bother. I like to get my mail delivered the same way everybody else gets theirs."

Melinda gave up the argument and turned over the outgoing packet to Wally Meecham and stepped back into the house and laid the incoming batch of mail on the table by her front door. Melinda's car was parked at the curbside, and the two walked together, exchanging pleasantries. The courteous mailman closed the gate and Melinda's car door before the two went their separate ways.

After the tobacco curing season ended, action at the farm shifted from scattered fields and curing barns to the cluster of packhouses that surrounded the main house. Any building that served as a place where tobacco could be stored during the barning and grading seasons qualified to be called a packhouse. These so-called packhouses became staging areas or workshops for the next phase in the seemingly endless chain of labor-intensive processes. Grading and tying followed. Each of the hundreds of thousands of individual tobacco leaves from the barns had to be hand sorted leaf by leaf into grades before the finished product could go to the market.

The sticks of cured tobacco had been packed away just as Dove and the others had looped them. The looping horses from the curing barns were also moved to the packhouses. And the process of looping was now reversed. This step was called "taking off," the one job that the boys on the farm would fight over. There was an unwritten rule that the boy who took off the tobacco could keep the string. Used tobacco twine was the main ingredient used in the manufacturing of homemade baseballs.

Except for the "taking off," adults only was the rule at the grading bench. Tobacco grading was yet another critical phase of product marketing. Leaves were individually and carefully hand sorted into grades ranging from lemon to trash. In-between grades included red, orange, yellow and green. As the sorting was being done by a grader, yet another specialty was called for, "tying" tobacco into bundles. Tying called for a different and very special talent.

Ten to twelve leaves of sorted tobacco would be collated and tied into a bundle. This process began in a manner somewhat similar to the looping process with the leaf stem ends perfectly aligned. However, instead of looping with tobacco twine, graded bundle heads would be tied with a "tie" leaf. Tie leaves were selected for esthetic qualities: no dark spots or worm holes. These "perfect" leaves would be wrapped tightly around the stem end of each bundle. When properly done, the tie leaf ends would not only be hidden, but the tying process created the illusion of a manufactured product. A properly tied bundle had a head that looked very similar to that of a whisk broom. Tender love and care and many hours of tedious work were devoted to this operation, not like the tobacco of later decades that is now

68

machine-harvested. In the contemporary version, the leaves are barned loose in huge pans; looping and tying are no longer required. The loose leaves are piled onto trays and placed in a forced-air, thermostatically controlled oven. No more looping, grading, taking off or tying. The Doves, Uncle Franks and Jubal Scotts are no longer around. The Burma Shave signs along the tobacco field roads are gone, too. That's ok though, because there's simply not enough people around that part of the state these days to read them anyhow.

In 1941 grading was time consuming and tedious, but no one complained. Payday came once a year on the tobacco farm, and grading was the last hurdle in the long and tricky process of turning a profit. Once the tobacco was taken off the sticks, there wasn't much for the children to do. They were allowed to romp and play as long as they stayed in sight of the packhouse. On the Fallston farm this meant playing in Jubal's yard.

The arrival of the mailman during these play periods would set the children off in a quarter-mile race to the boxes. During this one time of year, tobacco farm families received sales ads, promotions and catalogs on a scale that would rival today's junk mail. Volumes of duplicate mail filled each of the five mailboxes at the Fallston farm stop. But not this day. Master Jubal Scott received a personal letter.

A week had passed since the funeral. The boy ran to his room. From his window he could see the graders and children leaving for their noon meal. Aunt Sarah would be calling him any minute. Jubal's hands were sweating and dirty, but he couldn't wait; he could count all the letters he'd ever gotten with the fingers of one hand. Jubal tore open the letter totally destroying the envelope and read.

August 14, 1941

Dear Jubal,

I am pleased that you attended the funeral of my late husband, but I am also disappointed that I did not get to meet you personally at that time. Everyone tells me that you are a very handsome young man. From seeing your picture in the

69

papers, I am sure they are right about that. More importantly, I understand that you were my husband's friend. I would like for you to be my friend too. I know that this is a busy time on the farm for you and your folks, but I would count it a personal favor if you (and your parents) would be kind enough to allow me a short visit sometime in the near future. Any convenient time for you and your folks will be fine for me. I will be equally pleased if you have an opportunity to visit me. In either case, I look forward to hearing from you soon.

Yours truly,
Melinda Brandon

4368 Eastern Avenue
Centerville, North Carolina
Phone 784-K

P. S. If it could be arranged, I would like very much to meet and speak with Mr. Frank Ruffin. I understand Mr. Ruffin works for your father. Perhaps your father would be kind enough to arrange this also.

Jubal found Uncle Frank and read the letter to him.
"Do you know whut I think dis letter means?"
"You think we're in a heapa trouble, ain't that right?"
"Well dat depends on who you mean by WE," and whut you mean by heapa trouble."
"I mean you and me, that's the WE. And, specially ME. Papa's gonna kill me when he finds out about that watch. And I don't exactly think Papa's gonna be real pleased with you either."
"You know whut I think?" Uncle Frank asked.
"I thought we just went through all that. What's the matter with you now?"
"Hit ain't only you and me boy, hits yo pappy dats in considerable trouble, too."
"Papa? Why? What's he done?"

"He done told you to keep quiet 'bout dat whisky. Dat man Lacy was one of dem hardshell Baptist deacons. Mr. Lacy Brandon ain't been drinkin' no liquor."

"I still don't follow you," Jubal complained.

"Dat woman gone want to know everything. She ain't only gone want to know whut you seen, she's gwine want to know whut you smelled."

"How do you know that? You ain't never even seen this woman. She might not even ask me 'bout no watch. She knows that her husband's watch was on him when he died. She'll probably bring it along to show us. Just so long as she don't ask me about no watch, I'm keeping my mouth shut. Maybe Papa won't even make me answer her letter. He left that funeral procession awful fast like I told you. Remember?"

"Sho, I rememer you tellin' Sarah and me dat. But dat don't mean you papa or none of us gone keep dis woman fom findin' out de truth. De truth is gone come out iffn de Lawd want hit to come out. De good books says dat de rocks gone tell de truth if de Lawd wants de truth knowed."

Jubal and Uncle Frank had not been on the same page until suddenly the boy remembered reading in the Bible where Jesus actually said something about the rocks shouting. To date, Mason Scott had shown little or no interest in the explosion. Jubal thought, "Uncle Frank is right. Papa ain't going to do nothing. He's the world champion of staying out of other people's business."

Jubal became so convinced that his father would not be interested in the letter that he was tempted to hide the letter in his room. "After all," he rationalized, "that letter was addressed to me, wasn't it?" But Jubal finally decided that hiding the letter stood a larger chance of getting him deeper into trouble than keeping him out. He read the letter again. There was something about the tone of it that made him realize that widow Brandon was not going to take "no" for his answer. So he held the letter to his chest, said a prayer over the smudged epistle and laid it on the table with his father's pile of advertisements.

71

Chapter 14: The Confession

Jubal's gamble was winning. A month passed, and his father showed no sign of inviting the widow Brandon to visit them. Autumn happiness settled in and around the farm. Tobacco markets in the area opened, and the golden belt tobacco leaves were bringing top prices. Aunt Sarah baked a cake for Jubal's tenth birthday, and the children on the farm gave him a party. The boy's father was not at home at the time of the party; he apparently took no notice of his son's birthday. School started. Most of Jubal's classmates and other kids at school had not seen him since the explosion, and the boy became a celebrity all over again. Jubal liked the attention and indulged himself in the autumn joys around him. Tobacco was selling at prices far above expectations, and the money meant happy times on the farm. Jubal gave no further thought to Mrs. Brandon's letter.

Then one evening when the Scotts were eating their supper on the last Friday of September, Mason Scott told his son that Mrs. Brandon had phoned and was planning to visit to them Sunday afternoon. This news gave the boy a sick feeling in the pit of his stomach. And when he learned the real reason for her visit, that pain spread quickly to his head.

"I don't want you two involved in the mess about the explosion, but that woman," Mason Scott announced with emphasis on "that," she's convinced that her husband's death was not an accident. She's been pestering the heck out of the railroad, the state police, the newspapers, and Bob Dunbar in particular. Now, she's got those other two widows upset, and they're demanding a full-scale investigation. Mrs. Brandon is coming here in person. She's planning to give you and Uncle Frank the third degree."

"What's the third degree? I haven't gotten my first degree yet."

"Listen, boy, if you think you're going to joke your way through this business, you'd better think again. Bob Dunbar has been smack in the middle of the ruckus she's raising, and he's is beginning to believe that those women might be right. Bob is one of the few real friends I have in this world. So, for Bob's sake, I finally did what I should have done in the first place. I told him that you smelled whiskey on the man that grabbed you. Bob is plenty upset about that. Lacy Brandon, according to every person Bob has talked to, never even tasted whiskey in his whole life. Mrs. Brandon doesn't know about your whiskey smelling yet. But when she finds out, there's going to be plenty of fireworks. I'm hearing that this woman is a real tigress when her dander is up. If there's anything that you or Uncle Frank know that either of you haven't told me or Bob Dunbar, now is the time."

Jubal honestly didn't know what the third degree meant, but he did know that he was getter sicker by the second. He began to search for a spot where he could throw up and not have to clean up later. The boy had, become an expert at picking the right spots for vomiting. His father asked, "Are you all right? You look terrible."

Mason came over to the boy and laid his hand on the boy's forehead.

"It's just one of my ole sick headaches working on me. I gotta go lay down."

"OK, but we've gotta talk the minute you're up to it."

As the boy reached the dining room door he stopped. Uncle Frank's lecture about everything having its own time came into his aching head. Mason Scott knew the tell-tale signs. He knew that his son was sick, and even Mason Scott tended to be sympathetic when he saw his son in such agony.

"Maybe we'd better talk now," Jubal said. "There are two things I haven't told you."

The boy leaned against the door frame and told his father about the headlights.

"I'd just forget that, son. Chances are there were no headlights. I've had the same thing happen to me. You see and imagine all sorts of things when you're working those barns in the middle of the night. No, I'd just forget the headlights. You go on to bed now. We can talk later."

"There's something else, Papa. I took the man's watch."

"You did what?"

74

"I took the man's pocket watch."

"Why? How? What are you talking about?"

"When the man grabbed me, the back of my hand got caught between my body and something hard he was carrying in the bib pocket of his overalls. He was real strong and he wouldn't let me move my hand. He squeezed me so hard that for days the back of my hand was a big blue bruise. I kicked and carried on, but he didn't seem to notice or care that he was hurting me or that I might be hurting him. Anyway, when I finally managed to flip my hand over he probably didn't notice that either. But, my hand was hurting so bad, I had to do something. Now, with my hand loose, I could deal with the thing that had been hurting me. I worked my fingers into the man's overall bib pocket and wrapped them around the thing.

"The thing turned out to be the man's pocket watch. When the man suddenly let me go, the watch sorta came out and into my hand. The strap holding it must have snapped or slipped off or something. All I know is that I snatched like I had never snatched anything before in my whole life.

"Once I realized what I had in my hand, I intended to smash the thing against a tree for him hurting and scaring me the way he did. But, by the time Uncle Frank got there and the man let me go, I guess I just forgot all about the man's watch."

"Was there a chain or a string holding his watch? You said something about a strap."

"Yes, sir, it felt more like a shoestring. I snatched and wound up with the thing in my hand. I don't know what happened to anything but the watch."

"I take it from what you're saying, there was no string or anything attached to the watch when you gave it back to the man?" That was the question the boy had been dreading.

"I didn't give it back."

"What are you talking about? All three of the dead men on the locomotive had their watches. That was in the papers. You didn't take it to him. He came back for it. That's it, isn't it?"

"No, sir. He never came back. I wanted to take it back to him, but Uncle Frank wouldn't let me; he said it was too dangerous. The man warned me not to come to the train,

75

remember? I tried to take it back. I wanted to take it back but Uncle Frank wouldn't let me, Papa."

"I know you're sick, but for heaven's sakes quit talking in circles and just tell me how Brandon got his watch back."

"I've been trying to tell you, Papa, the man didn't get his watch back. We still have it."

"We? Who is we?"

"Well, er, er Uncle Frank has it." Somehow implicating Uncle Frank was making the boy feel better. After all, Uncle Frank was an adult. And, didn't the newspaper reporter write that Mr. Frank Ruffin was in charge?

"I might have known you'd get that poor old man in on this somehow," Mason snapped.

Now Jubal and his father were both sick. Mason was holding his head and groaning, while Jubal made a mad dash across the side porch and threw up into the shrubbery. His father ran past him into the yard. As he passed, he said, "After you get Uncle Frank up here, get yourself in the bed. I'm going to find Bob Dunbar. We have more explaining to do than I thought."

He stopped and waited while the boy vomited again.

"Is there anything else? You two didn't happen to blow up that engine, did you?"

"No, sir," the boy answered weakly.

"Who else knows about the watch business?"

"Just Uncle Frank."

"You'd better make darn sure you keep it that way. Both your lives might depend on it. I'm going to find Sheriff Bob. You find Uncle Frank. I want to see you, him and that watch right here when we get back. Do you understand me?"

Chapter 15: The Evidence

The boy was feeling better by the time his father cleared the yard. He would much more have preferred an ordinary killer to go after him than his own father. He ran and found Uncle Frank talking to one of the mules and broke up that conversation in a hurry. Jubal announced his news and his father's proclamation. Jubal was pale and weak now. He paused, looking into Uncle Frank's eyes expecting the old man to show similar signs of alarm and distress. Seeing none, he asked, "Well, what are we going to do now?"

"Listen, Jube, whatever happened dat night wuz partly yo fault and partly yo Uncle Frank's dat's fo sho. But de good Lawd put both us deah at dem barns dat night fur some purpose more'n jus curing bacca. Now hit looks like we gwine find out what dat purpose wus. Most folks never find out why de Lawd allow us to do dis and dat, why some folks get sick while other folks is healthy, but befoe dis business is ovah, I got a fellin' we gone know everything bout dis heah business. Hits gwine be all right, Jube. You just mind whut yo pappy says and don't be lettin' no strangers in on dis watch business."

"Aren't you worried, scared?"

"I'ze fraid some for you, Jube. But not fo mysef. When yo live long as ole Uncle Frank, de Lawd teaches yo to not be 'fraid for yosef no mo. Now boy, yo jus truss de good Lawd and do yo best, and He gone take care of yo too. Like hit or no, yo pappy is in dis thing wid us. He done as bad as you and me when he didn't truss yo bout de whiskey smell. De good Lawd knows dat yo pappy, like everybody else, needs sum fixen too."

The boy didn't understood all of Uncle Frank's sermon, but it did have a calming effect. The real reason for Jubal's return to health, however, came from the fact that he had confessed his sins to his father and lived to tell someone about it.

Uncle Frank and Jubal had not been waiting long when they saw two clouds of dust heading their way. Seconds later, Mason Scott, closely followed by the sheriff, were both parked in the Scotts' front yard. There were no preliminaries; this was official business. After entering the parlor and shutting the door behind them, Uncle Frank wordlessly surrendered the watch. He delivered it to the sheriff in a small Golden Grain tobacco pouch. At the cost of a nickel, that small pouch originally contained enough tobacco to roll twenty cigarettes, plus the papers to roll them on and directions for rolling them. The present contents of the sack, however, was something else.

Sheriff Dunbar took the pouch. He loosened the draw string, opened the neck of the sack and gently nudged the watch into the palm of his hand. Then he pointed the watch in Jubal's direction and asked, "Is this the watch you took from the railroad man?" Jubal walked over and looked at the watch.

"Yes, sir." The room was quiet. Jubal thought he heard the thing ticking, but he knew better. The ticking sound was the pounding in his fast beating heart.

Jubal's father was staring at the watch and shaking his head from side to side as if in disbelief. He seemed to be in another world, his usual own silent world. The sheriff became impatient, waiting for Jubal's father to tell them what was upsetting him. Finally, Mason turned to his son and instead of enlightening the group, said, "Go ahead, Jube, why don't you tell the sheriff what you told me?" The boy hesitated. After a long pause, Mason noticed that the boy was waiting for double permission before testifying to the county sheriff. Mason said, "Go ahead, son, start with the part about the headlights across the tracks. Tell Sheriff Dunbar everything you told me earlier."

Jubal spilled out everything, including the car lights, whiskey smell and the man's watch. Sheriff Dunbar asked Frank Ruffin if he could add anything.

"Naw, suh, hit happened pretty much de way Jube 'scribed it. I knowed right off dat Jube didn't like de man, but I passed hit off dat he done scairt de boy hafta death. Couse, I wuz nervous and outta breath too.   Fact is, all of us, 'cludin de man acted scairt and nervous."

Meanwhile, Mason Scott continued to stare at the watch. "This looks like an official railroad watch, doesn't it?"

"Yep, that's a nice looking watch all right," the sheriff agreed.

"That watch is a piece of junk," Mason announced with authority.

"What makes you say a dumb thing like that?" the sheriff wanted to know.

"I know because, unless this happens to be my own watch, and I pray that it isn't, I've got one just like it up in my room, that's why."

"You're joking, and I haven't heard you make a joke in years," the sheriff exclaimed.

"I hate to spoil your fun, Sheriff, but this is no joke. Hold your horses. I'll be back in a minute."

Sure enough, in less than a minute Mason Scott returned with a watch in his outstretched hand. The sheriff held his hand out and the four of them looked down on the two identical timepieces. Each had the majestic steam engine roaring across its face, the same stream of black smoke billowing across the sky in opposite directions.

"Where in tarnation did you get a watch just like this one?" the sheriff wanted to know.

"I worked at the railroad shop in Centerville when I was in my late teens and early twenties. We went out on strike in 1926. The strike lasted over a year and I never went back. While I was working there one of the car repairers ordered one of these watches from a catalog. The thing was cheap, but as you see, a great looking watch. In fact they look even better than a real railroad watch. Most of the shop men who saw it, including me, just had to have one. These watches created a fad like you wouldn't believe. Hundreds of us ordered these watches during the days and months before the strike. Like most everything that looked too good to be true, these watches turned out to be real duds. And I see this one isn't working either."

"Did you notice if this watch was working when you took it, Jube?"

"That's one of the things I did right away. I guess that's one of the reasons I thought about throwing it away. It wasn't working and I was afraid I might have broken the thing. When I noticed that it had stopped on 8:15 I figured it was broke before I

79

ever touched it. See, that's the same time on it now, just like I found it," Jubal answered.

"Within no time my watch quit working, too, just like this one," Jubal's father continued. "And from what I heard, everybody else had about the same luck. Those watches are just plain no good. Mine stayed in the shop more than it did in my pocket. Finally, I got tired of paying to have the thing fixed. I threw it in a drawer years ago, and it's been there ever since."

"Well, this is an unexpected piece of luck. This may lead to something." Turning to Jubal and Uncle Frank, the sheriff asked, "Have either of you had the back off this watch?"

"No sir," they both answered.

"Dat timepiece done been in my possession since I took it from Jube on de night of dat explosion. Naw, suh, hit ain't been open," Frank Ruffin added.

"Good," the sheriff countered. "This at least gives us something to work on. I know a good watch man that I can trust. I'll get him to check it and see what he might be able to tell us. Meanwhile, we have two ways we can go. One, you can refuse to allow widow Brandon's visit. That will keep her from questioning Jube and Uncle Frank. She has no legal grounds for talking to them. There has been no proof that a crime was committed and there is no official investigation under way. In the meantime, I can continue to chase down the leads we have on my own. For instance, I can find out what kind of clothes Brandon was wearing that night. Maybe the man didn't even own a pair of bib overalls."

"What do you think will happen if Mrs. Brandon comes here and questions Uncle Frank and Jube?" Mason asked.

"I was coming to that," the sheriff continued. "I think letting her visit is the right thing to do. By cooperating, we'll likely get some of our own questions answered a lot sooner and easier, too. For instance, she probably knows exactly what her husband was wearing that night, and she would certainly know if this is her husband's watch. You see what I mean?"

"Why not let her come here on Sunday then?" Mason asked.

"Because, the other side of this business is that we don't know enough about this woman yet. We do know that she's a woman on a mission and she has nothing to lose. She's already lost her husband. All hell may well break loose, too, when she finds out that the man who grabbed Jube was not her husband."

"Yeah, sure, I see what you're getting at," Mason Scott agreed.

"She finds out what we know when she comes Sunday and maybe it's in all the papers on Monday morning. You know what that could mean?"

"Yeah, you're right," Mason replied." Jube and Uncle Frank could be in a great deal of danger."

"Exactly."

"Do you know anything about the preacher at Brandon's church?" Mason asked.

"Nothing. Why do you want to know about him? What's he got to do with this?" the sheriff asked.

"We could talk to him first. He can likely tell us whether Mrs. Brandon can be trusted to cooperate with us or not."

"Well, that's up to you. You know a lot more about Baptist preachers than I do. We can give him a call now and see if you can see him in private tonight or tomorrow."

"We'd better not call on our phone," Mason suggested. "Everybody on our party line would be wondering and speculating about what we want to see the preacher in Centerville about."

"OK," the sheriff agreed. "You come with me. You can make the phone call from my office."

As Mason reached the door, he asked, "Is there anything else you two have to say before the sheriff leaves?"

In response to their "No, sirs," Mason again warned them not to talk about this to a living soul, and he instructed Uncle Frank to look after Jubal until he got back. "Like it or not, we're all in this mess together. And we're gonna have to stick together until we get ourselves out."

For the first time, the boy realized that he may be in danger. But with his father, Sheriff Bob and Uncle Frank looking after him, Jubal Scott was not afraid.

"By the way, Uncle Frank," Mason said, "I think it's best at this point to tell Aunt Sarah everything that we know. After all, there is an element of danger here, and she deserves to know what's going on. Just tell her to keep it in this house, OK?"

"Yas, suh," Uncle Frank said, "I 'preciate dat, Mr. Mason. I'll tell her."

Chapter 16: The Widow's Visit

Mrs. Brandon's preacher, Mason learned by phone, just happened to be attending a Baptist meeting in Martin on Saturday morning. That fortunate happenstance provided the opportunity for secrecy that Mason hoped for.

The Reverend Robert Turner also turned out to be more than Mason expected. Having spent his church life in tiny Baptist churches, Mason Scott was expecting a facsimile of former pastors he'd known. Robert Turner did not fit this mold. He was young, casual and candid.

Mason's main concern remained. He worried that in a larger church like Mill Creek, the pastor may not be personally acquainted with each individual member, namely Melinda Brandon. That concern evaporated quickly when Mason Scott learned that had counseled both Melinda and Lacy Brandon following Collins' death. The pastor said to Mason Scott, "Before I answer your question about Melinda Brandon, let me tell you about her husband. Lacy Brandon was the finest Christian gentleman I've ever had the privilege of knowing. Aside from his high moral character, Lacy Brandon was also smart. Lacy Brandon would be the last person on earth who'd be a party to something as dumb and stupid as putting cold water into a red hot boiler. Now about Melinda. First off, I knew that she was planning to visit you tomorrow afternoon before you called me. Believe me, Melinda Brandon is as good as her word. And her word is based upon her unshakeable belief in the almighty. Do you get my drift? Trust her completely and help her. That is my advice and counsel."

Melinda Brandon called John Russell and asked if she might take her car down to his garage. She told Russell that she was planning to drive to Fallston on Sunday and she might need a new battery. "One of the teachers at school had to give me a jump start yesterday after school. Maybe I just left my lights on or something. The thing started right up just a minute ago. I've got the motor running now. But there's some awful lonely territory between here and Fallston. I wouldn't want to walk down that road by myself."

"If you're not here in two minutes, I'll come looking for you." John Russell promised.

Jubal and his father went to Sunday school and church as usual the next morning at the Fallston Baptist Church. Aunt Sarah had dinner ready when the pair reached home. After dinner Jubal went upstairs to his room. From the vantage point of his front window Jubal would be able to see Mrs. Brandon long before she could see him. The boy was used to spending time alone in his room. One of his favorite games was studying the traffic, such as it was, that passed his house. He prided himself on being able to recognize and identify the locals from great distances. Luckily, the crops on Jubal's side of the road this year were cotton and peanuts. The taller corn on the other side would have obscured his view.

He set his clock in the window so that he could see the time without diverting his attention from the road. Jubal's game was not as fast paced as Ataris'. Mrs. Brandon was due to arrive at two p.m. Between 1:43 and 1:54 the road remained empty. At 1:55 a car unfamiliar to him appeared on the boy's horizon. He knew it was the widow's.

Stopping at the mailboxes, she read the names before turning into the lane to Jubal's house. She was driving a late-model Chevy that was cleaner than all the neighborhood cars except Miss Parsons'. He moved from the front to a side window and watched her get out of her car. While he was keeping an eagle eye on her, she was taking a careful look at her surroundings. She didn't seem to be in a hurry. Jubal was totally surprised when the widow Brandon looked up. The windows in their old house reached almost to the floor.

Jubal was standing stock still, in full view from his knees up. Melinda Brandon looked directly at him and smiled and waved. Panic, disbelief and wonder consumed the surprised boy. He was totally unprepared for that moment. Although surprise was a factor, the greeting or even the way she looked at him was not what stunned the boy. Melinda Brandon bore a striking

84

resemblance to a woman in the photograph that the boy kept hidden in his dresser.

Mason Scott had ordered his son to wait in his room until called. Minutes turned into an hour before the invitation came. He was wondering what they could be talking about for such a long time. A bit of forethought would have provided Jubal an easy answer. There were two people in the picture that Jubal had secretly hidden: his parents. Jubal had no memory of his mother as the beautiful woman in that photograph. But his father did. If the boy was mesmerized by the ghost of his mother's picture, what must have happened to his father when he saw the incarnation of his beautiful Belle?

By the time Jubal finally entered the parlor, Aunt Sarah had delivered a tray containing coffee, lemonade, cookies and blackberry cobbler. The room smelled good and it wasn't only the aroma of the food. Mrs. Brandon arose from the sofa and walked toward the boy as he entered the room.

Everything that was happening seemed unreal to the boy. He was half expecting to wake up and discover that none of this was really happening: it must be a dream. At best, from this lovely stranger, the boy was expecting at most a courteous handshake. She held out her arms and Jubal walked into them. She was warm, soft and wonderful. She hugged the boy and held him close. She felt and smelled wonderful. She was real. Jubal was struggling to keep from crying or laughing, he wasn't sure which.

When she finally let the boy go, he said, "I'm sorry about your husband, and I'm sorry I didn't answer your letter."

"I'm sure all of this has been very difficult for you, Jubal. There's no need to apologize. All I want is for us to be friends from now on. Have we got a deal?"

"Yes, ma'am," he said and meant it.

"Come sit here with me and tell me all about yourself," she said.

The boy had completely forgotten about his father and everything else, until Mason Scott spoke. "I'll leave you two to get acquainted while I go down and fetch Uncle Frank. Mrs. Brandon would like to meet him too."

Jubal looked at his father. What he saw was much more than he had become accustomed to seeing.   At that moment, Mason Scott looked more like the man in the picture than the boy had ever noticed before. That photograph, supposedly of both his parents, was also, supposedly, taken a year before Jubal was born.   Mrs. Brandon looked very strikingly like the woman in that picture. Jubal's mother had been sick since the boy's earliest recollections. He was never fully convinced that anyone could have ever been as beautiful as that picture portrayed his mother to be. Those doubts were now dispelled. He also thought he'd figured out for the very first time how and why his father had become the loneliest man in the world.

The boy was giddy from her closeness, and he was in a silly mood. As invited to do, Jubal commenced to tell the beautiful widow all about himself. He let his imagination run rampant, leaping from one subject to the next and stretching the truth well beyond its limits. He told her he was the smartest boy in school. He was also the greatest at fishing, swimming, reading, baseball and everything in between. He even threw in some of the stuff Uncle Frank had told about Fallston in the old days, never pausing long enough to give Uncle Frank any of the credit. He told about finding arrowheads around the old Indian mounds and digging up bucketfuls of bullets right here on the farm. He told exaggerated stories about the old Confederate fort on the river. He cited incorrectly that the rebels used cannons to sink dozens of Yankee boats during the Civil War. Then suddenly right in the middle of the ramblings, the boy blurted the question that was really occupying his mind.

"Do you have any children?"

"No, I don't."

There was sadness in her voice that made the boy sad, too. Although Jubal was enormously relieved and pleased with her answer, he hated himself for the pain he'd just caused her. He was thinking, "Well, you can have me." There followed an awkward moment when neither of them seemed to know how to continue.

However, their embarrassing hiatus was cut short by the return of Jubal's father, Uncle Frank and Sheriff Dunbar.

Melinda Brandon had never seen Uncle Frank before, but she had spoken to the sheriff by phone on several occasions. With the widow's permission, Mason had called the sheriff and asked him to join them.

Uncle Frank and the sheriff were introduced and each expressed condolences. Mrs. Brandon congratulated Uncle Frank on his fame as a master teller of stories. "Mr. Scott has told me so much about the two of you, I feel that I have known both of you for a long time."

The next words the lovely widow spoke let everyone in the room know that she had not come to pay them a social visit.

"Gentlemen, I hope that this doesn't come as a shock to you, but I am here today because I do not believe that my husband's death was an accident. About this time last year, as you have probably heard or read, there was a tragic accident at the railroad shop in Centerville. A pipefitter named Harry Collins was crushed to death while working underneath a passenger car. The car that Collins was working under had been temporarily shifted onto a siding and was scheduled to be moved into the regular repair shops at Centerville sometime during that day.

"My husband was the conductor of the switch engine crew assigned to move that car. Railroad repairmen, such as carpenters, electricians and pipefitters, working on any rolling stock subject to being moved, are required to post flags: one flag on each end of a car, or coupled string of cars as the case may be, before doing work on said rolling stock."

Melinda Brandon had memorized this from her husband's rule book.

"These flags, once posted, are sacred," she explained. "A repairman's flag once it is set, cannot be removed by any person other than the person who placed that flag or flags. If an engine crewman, even though they have orders to move said rolling stock, encounters a workman's flag, that crewman is required to locate the person who actually set the flag. The person who posted the flags, and only the person who set them has the authority to remove them. A flagged car simply cannot be moved until this procedure has been satisfactorily completed.

"According to my husband's sworn testimony, there was no flag posted at the end of the passenger car as he and his crew approached it. There was a pipefitter's flag found later posted on the opposite end, no argument there, but to this day the second flag, the one which would have saved Harry Collins' life has not been found."

She paused. Jubal couldn't tell if she needed to regain her composure, or whether she wanted to see if all of them were absorbing what she was saying. After a lengthy pause, she asked politely, "Shall I continue?"

"Yes, yes," all answered.

"During the investigation which followed, several shopmen testified that they had seen the flag, the flag that would have obviously prevented this terrible tragedy, in place only minutes before my husband's switch engine arrived on the scene. The members of my husband's crew, however, backed my husband's testimony. To a man, his crew swore that no flag was ever seen. As you know, Centerville is a railroad town. Thousands of men work there in the huge repair shops. Unfortunately, many of these men, until this day, believe that my husband or one of his crew removed that flag. My husband was in charge that night. Therefore, because of this responsibility, he was blamed by many for that terrible accident.

"As I have already stated, the flag has not been found. I am here today to speak for my dear dead husband. Lacy Brandon was a good and honest man. He would neither remove a worker's flag or lie to protect any member of his crew for removing it. Yet, my husband was ridiculed mercilessly and ultimately demoted and even killed for doing something that he would never do or never condone. Since the death of Mr. Collins, my husband was reassigned to duty as a brakeman on the most obscure jobs the railroad could find. And now, my husband and the other members of that crew are dead. I believe that my husband and the others were killed as payback for the death of Harry Collins. I believe that those three men were executed for a crime that they did not commit."

Mrs. Brandon was softly sobbing. There was an awkward minute or so while she blew her nose and struggled with her emotions. When she spoke again, her voice was once again clear and composed.

"I would be very grateful if you people would tell me everything you remember about the pulpwood train the night my husband and the others were killed. For my part, I have given Mr. Scott here my word that I will cooperate in every way with Sheriff Dunbar and you people here in this room. I also promise you that I will treat anything you say as off-the-record, confidential, privileged information not to be repeated or used without your permission."

The boy wasn't sure about off-the-record, confidential, privileged information and stuff like that, so he looked at his father, who responded by saying, "It's OK, son, go ahead. Start at the beginning and tell Mrs. Brandon exactly what you did, what you saw and what you heard."

"Everything?"

"Yes, son, everything,"

It took the boy about five minutes to tell his story. Mrs. Brandon listened intently and did not interrupt, holding held her questions until Jubal finished. Then she asked, "Are you positive that the man was wearing bib overalls?"

"Yes, ma'am."

"You're sure that you smelled whiskey on that man's breath and clothing?"

"Yes, ma'am."

"There's no way you could be mistaken about either the overalls or the whiskey?"

"Well, about the whiskey maybe I could be wrong. If it wasn't whiskey I smelled, it must've been something almost like it. But the bib overalls, yes, ma'am, I'm sure. That's where the watch was, and we've got the watch here to prove it. I'm real sure about that. Don't you believe me?"

"Oh yes, yes, yes Jubal, I believe you. I believe every word you've said. It's just that these questions are so very, very important. You see, my husband never owned a pair of bib overalls during the fifteen years we were married. And, to my knowledge, my husband did not own or carry a second watch. And I never knew him to touch alcohol in any way shape or form. Do you all see what this means? The man who grabbed and held you that night was not my husband!   If he wasn't my husband, who was he? And what was he doing at the site of the explosion, at the time of the explosion?"

"Maybe it was one of the other crewmen. Maybe Jube and Uncle Frank got their names mixed up" the sheriff offered.

"Jim Spencer, the fireman, was a small man, not nearly as large as yourself, Mr. Scott. The other big firemen used to poke fun at Jim because of his size. They called him Sparky. Back in the days before stokers, coal had to be manually shoveled into the firebox. The joke was that one day when Jim was late for work, someone said he must have thrown himself into the firebox along with his shovel and turned himself into a spark. The man who held you was big and tall. Is that right, Jubal?" Melinda Brandon was in a much lighter mood now.

"Yes, ma'am, he was much bigger than my father."

"What about King? Could it have been him?"

"George King was a big man all right. Before the Collins thing, George was a highly respected engineer.   But, unfortunately, George King was also a cripple. The man could barely walk. For the last several years of his life, once George was in the engineer's seat, that's where George stayed. He suffered terribly from arthritis and had to be helped into his seat in his cab. George's physical condition was the reason cited by the railroad for assigning him to runs like the pulpwood run here to Fallston. He, like my husband and Jim Spencer, had become railroad outcasts. No. I assure you that the man you've described was definitely not a member of that locomotive crew."

"What do you think happened?" Mason asked.

"I believe that someone other than Lacy's crew caused that engine to explode. I honestly don't have any idea how anyone could have done that. I still believe that my husband, Jim Spencer and George King were murdered. I believed that even before I came here today. Thanks to Jubal and Uncle Frank, I am convinced beyond a shadow of doubt that someone else other than the crew of that locomotive was responsible for that explosion. Once the murderers realized that there was someone at that tobacco barn that night, they had to cook up a scheme to

90

keep them away. That plan almost worked until now. Thanks to us getting together here today, every person in this room now knows that someone else was down there at the time of that explosion."

"All right," the sheriff responded, "so now we know that someone else was down there that night. That's a long ways from proving that that person or persons actually took part in a crime. Maybe these people just happened to be in the wrong place at the wrong time and got the heck out of there when the locomotive blew up."

"You can keep on maybeing forever Bob, but the picture Jubal and Uncle Frank just described to us doesn't fit any of those maybes. Whoever the man was that grabbed Jubal, that man had foreknowledge that that locomotive was going to blow up." Mason found himself disagreeing with his best friend.

"You're right, Mason, I honestly don't know what to make of it," Sheriff Dunbar answered. "But one thing's for sure: We aren't going to rest until we find out what really happened down there that night. Thanks to you, Mrs. Brandon, and you, Jubal, and you, Uncle Frank, we probably know much more than those men think we know. That's what we want them to go on thinking until we can figure some way to identify them and find out what they were doing there. We believe that someone else was there. We have hard evidence there was someone else at the scene of the explosion. We must also assume that we may be dealing with cold-blooded killers. We simply can't be too careful. I hope no one followed you here today. If these people are killers and knew what we now know, Jubal and Uncle Frank would be in great danger."

"Do you think anyone followed you here today?" Mason asked Mrs. Brandon.

"No one followed Mrs. Brandon today," Jubal answered for her.

"How do you know that?" Mason snapped.

"Well, at least for the first hour that Mrs. Brandon's been here they didn't. I was watching from my window. Only six cars came by here or were in sight during that hour, and I recognized all of those."

91

"Good work, Jubal," Melinda Brandon responded. "That was good detective work and is very reassuring, Jubal."

Before Melinda Brandon left, Jubal volunteered to play detective again. He ran up to his room and searched the area for signs of strangers. He came back a couple of minutes later with the all-clear. The group had already decided in the meantime that Mrs. Brandon would return home by a different route.

Mrs. Brandon agreed to ease up on her efforts to solve the case for the time being, while the sheriff worked on the new leads. She gave Jubal another hug and shook hands with Mason, the sheriff and Uncle Frank.

"I don't know how all this is going to end, but you people have given me hope. And that's more than I had when I came here. Thank you all and God bless each of you."

Everyone walked the widow to her car. Mason Scott rushed ahead and opened the door.

"What's next? When will we see you again?" Mason asked.

"I really don't know," Melinda Brandon answered. "It depends on what the sheriff comes up with and when, I suppose. I hope something will happen soon. Thanks again for your help and hospitality. Tell Aunt Sarah to expect me for supper the next time. That blackberry cobbler of hers was out of this world."

"You've got a date," an embarrassed Mason Scott answered. His face was suddenly as red as the sunset.

She responded by offering her hand through the car window. Mason shook her hand ever so briefly. While Uncle Frank, Mason and the sheriff waved goodbyes from the yard, Jubal rushed upstairs and watched her all the way to Melton Springs.

Chapter 17: A Father and Son Talk

Except in the coldest, nastiest weather, Jubal preferred walking to school over spending more than two hours on the bus. However, the main reason that Jubal loved to walk was not a matter of time. About half of his one-mile foot route to school was on the farm, where he was joined by the black children from the tenant houses along the way. Jubal was the bag boy for goodies from Aunt Sarah. Three of the black children were Aunt Sarah's grandchildren, but she treated the farm's seven tenant children all equally. The time shared with the other farm kids was the happiest part of Jubal's school day. At the railroad tracks their paths would diverge. The black school was located two blocks south and just inside the tracks. Jubal's route led north along the tracks and finally through a stretch of woods, before ending in the playground behind the whites' schoolhouse.

The morning following Mrs. Brandon's visit, Jubal's father informed him that he was to ride the bus to and from school until further notice. The boy was especially looking forward to seeing the farm kids that particular morning. Aunt Sarah had assembled ham biscuits and cookies, a rare double treat. Ordinarily, Jubal did not challenge his father about anything, especially an order as clearly stated as this one. But that was yesterday and before Melinda Brandon's visit.

"Please, Papa, I want to walk, I er--- please Papa we need to walk, er, I mean talk." So much for Jubal's newfound assertiveness.

"What do 'we' need to walk or talk about, son?" his father snapped.

Jubal's father was as confused as the boy, but his offer to listen, even reluctantly, came as a pleasant surprise. "It's, it's about me, me riding the school bus." The boy finally managed to stammer.

Mason Scott was thinking that his son was about to argue against having to be the first pickup on the bus route because he didn't relish spending hours on the bus. He was not expecting the argument that his son now articulated.

The boy gathered himself and began confidently, "It's not that I don't like riding on the bus, Papa. I just like walking to school with the kids here on the farm, that's all. You probably don't know it, and I don't think their parents know it, but the kids all count on me. Aunt Sarah fixes treats for all of them almost every day. I take whatever Aunt Sarah fixes to the kids on my way. If I didn't take the stuff to them, they'd have to walk all the way up here to the house every morning. And they're all afraid of you. They don't think you'd like to see them up here every morning. And besides, they don't even have any way of knowing ahead of time if Aunt Sarah's got any goodies for them. So you see it really messes things up for them up when I ride the school bus. They'll think I don't want to be seen with them, or think that I'm tired of being their delivery boy. What am I supposed to tell them?"

"Tell them your father said for you to ride the bus. That's the truth."

"Then they'll think you don't want me to walk with them. Isn't that just about as bad? Nothing is going to happen to me with them around."

"Hey, you may be right, son. This situation is much more complicated than I thought. You're right, we can't let that explosion business run our lives. It's OK, you go on, walk today. We can talk more about this again tonight. But keep your eyes and ears open and don't linger in those woods back of the school and come straight home. You hear me?"

The man sounded like a real father. He was worried about his son and told him so. It was one of the nicest things the boy's father had ever said to him. That night, Mason Scott gave Jubal a policeman's whistle. Jubal promised to blow the thing if and when he felt threatened. And that was the end of the walking-to-school discussion. Jubal grew an inch on that one.

After supper, Mason sat Jubal down and gave an update on the watch investigation. At the outset the boy had high hopes that this meant that the case was about to be solved. His father began. "The watch you lifted from the stranger looks just like mine, we all said that. Remember?"

94

"Yes, sir, they looked exactly alike. I saw that much myself."

Mason then began a long and complicated monlogue. The boy soon realized that it was only out of frustration that his father had volunteered to explain something like this to him. Ordinarily Mason Scott would have said nothing. Jubal sensed that his father was trying to make something out of nothing. The whole discussion was completely out of character for Mason Scott. But he forged on. "You were wrong, son. We were all wrong. The watch you took from the man was practically brand new. None of us had a chance to see, but the workings inside are different from mine. The hour and minute hands are not exactly the same either. We should have picked up on that. Some detectives we are. Apparently, according to the watch company's advertisement I have here, the watch manufacturer has recently come out with a new and improved version of the watch I own.

"Bob Dunbar's jeweler friend says that the new watches are very similar to the one that I bought fifteen years ago. In other words, this new batch is no better than the first ones. Some things never change. According to the jeweler both are pieces of junk. I guess the watch company figured that the watch scam worked before, let's try it again. Given the track record of these watches and the fact that the man was still toting it, probably means that the man's watch had been working until very recently. Nobody carries a watch that won't work. That means that the watch you took from the man must have been purchased very recently. The bottom line is, nothing I've been able to find out has helped us very much."

"That's too bad," the boy said. He thought that the bottom line was the end. But his frustrated father wasn't finished.

"Bob Dunbar called the watch company and found out that they have sold more that two hundred of these new watches to customers in Centerville during the last six months alone. Thanks to Bob, we do have a list of those customers. That's an awful long list of suspects. And, there's no guarantee that our man is among them. What a mess!"

Jubal accepted his father's latest lament as an extension of his belief that his own existence was the cause of his unhappiness. The boy said to his already frustrated father, "It's all my fault, isn't it? If I hadn't taken that man's ole watch, we wouldn't be in this mess. Uncle Frank gets things mixed up sometimes, and everybody says I exaggerate. Nobody would have believed either of us without the watch. I wish that I'd a' just flung the darn thing in the river."

"And let killers go free in the bargain. Oh, no, no, son, I'm not saying that this is your fault at all. If it's anyone's fault, it's mine. You were at those barns that night because I told you to be there. I'm as stumped and depressed as you are. Somebody's getting away with murder, and nobody seems to be able to do anything about it. We've just got to figure some way to find out who these guys are and what they were up to. It's frustrating not knowing just what to do next. I'm as anxious as you are to get this business over and done with."

While his father's apology made the boy feel better, Jubal was thinking, "So you can ask Mrs. Brandon to come back here for supper. Right, Pop?" But, of course, he wouldn't dare say anything close to that. Instead he said, "I want this over with, too, Papa."

That night, alone in his room, the boy took a fresh look at their stale situation. He thought, "Thanks to the watch and Mrs. Brandon's story, several people now believe that somebody besides the crew of that locomotive was at the track about the same time that Brandon and the others died. But, because of the danger to me and Uncle Frank, our only real piece of evidence, namely the watch, is useless. In the meantime Mrs. Brandon, because of the danger to us, is avoiding us, too. This is one big crazy mixed-up mess I've gotten us into. It stinks."

The boy couldn't sleep. He began to wonder what this was doing to his father. Jubal turned on the light in his room and looked at his clock. It was three o'clock. He went downstairs on the chance that his father might be awake. Halfway down the stairs, the boy smelled coffee. Mason Scott was sitting at the kitchen table, cup in hand.

"Are you sick, son?" he asked.

96

"No, sir, I just can't sleep. I've been doing some thinking. I've thought of a plan for finding the man who owns that railroad watch."

"This sounds very interesting, son. Let's hear it."

"We can tell one of those newspaper writers that I found a railroad watch near the place where the locomotive exploded. That way, Sheriff Bob can set a trap. When the man I took the watch from shows up, Sheriff Bob will be waiting for him. You know, just like we saw in that movie at Martin a couple of weeks ago. I'm sure I'd recognize the man if I saw him again. I ain't afraid of him. No, sir, I've done faced him once, and I ain't scared to face him again."

The more the boy talked the bolder he became. As the words tumbled out, Jubal could see himself, like the cowboy that inspired his daring plan, riding off into the sunset on his stick horse. "Sheriff Bob will be waitin', -----"

That was it for Jubal's grand plan. "Let's get one thing straight right now." Just the tone of his father's voice was enough to yank the young hero off his stick horse. "I don't ever, ever want to hear this kind of talk from you again. Getting yourself killed is not the way this thing is going to be settled. Do you understand me?"

"Yes, sir. I understand, but I just want to get this thing over with."

"I know what you mean. I feel the same way. I couldn't sleep either. I've been trying to come up with a plan, too. I appreciate you wanting to help. You're a brave boy, and I don't doubt for a minute that you're willing to try a fool stunt like that, too. You're right about the watch. Without it I probably wouldn't have believed your story either. So, you just quit worrying about solving the case and keep your eye out for that man. This is not the movies, and you're the only son I've got. Hey, you've just given me an idea, son. I think I know a way to start getting answers instead of questions."

Jubal wondered what new idea he'd given his father. He intended to ask him right out, but what he was seeing took priority over what he was thinking or hearing. He thought he saw tears in his father's eyes. It was very late and bleary eyes could be easily mistaken for teary ones. Mason Scott continued to talk, but he turned away so that he wasn't facing his son. "I'm glad you came down, Jube. But, it's late and you have school in a little while." Mason Scott then did the most uncharacteristic thing he'd done in years. He turned and grabbed the boy and hugged him so hard that the boy almost cried out in pain. Jubal discovered that his father's body was made of steel. But the words, "I love you, son," took away the boy's pain in an instant.

Chapter 18:   The Diesel Comes to Fallston

Except for the father and son weekly trips to the movies on Saturday nights and church on Sundays, it was business as usual, and Jubal and his father were seldom together. The boy knew that his father had the farm business to look after. Nevertheless, Jubal fantasized that at any moment his father might burst into the house and announce that the case had been solved.   More realistically, however, he was hoping that his father would as least reveal his plan for solving the murder case. Weeks went by with the new Mason Scott being the old Mason Scott all over again, keeping his thoughts to himself and speaking only when necessary. Jubal was left alone to wonder and wait. Luckily, however, the boy had the good life on the farm to keep him occupied.

During these unsupervised days, Jubal used his position as boss' son. He helped out only when and where the work suited him. Jubal tried his hand at picking cotton, but the boy never got the knack in spite of the fact that he thought picking cotton looked like one of the simplest jobs in the world. Pull the little white puffs out of their shells, stuff them in a sack and get paid by the pound for the puffs in your sack. Jubal could never pick enough cotton to register on the field scales. His cotton picking was a joke, and he didn't like being laughed at. But Jubal could hold his own in the peanut gang.

Peanut harvest was a four-stage operation.   First stage: Loosen the soil around the root of the plant, the part containing the peanuts using a mule and plow.   Second stage: Erect haystack frames at even intervals throughout the peanut patch. The frames, shaped like upside-down crosses, served as racks for stacking the peanut plants. The third stage, Jubal's forte, called for getting the loosened plants out of the plowed ground and transferring them onto the nearest haystack. The third stage of the peanut harvest was a three-step operation: Yank, shake and fling. 1. Grab the plant by the foliage and yank the entire plant, peanut, roots and all, out of the ground.   2. Remove the dirt clinging to the root and peanuts by shaking the plant much the

99

way a dog removes imaginary fleas from a rag doll. 3. Take the peanut plant to the nearest haystack and fling it onto the haystack frame.

After a few weeks, the green peanut patch was transformed into a matrix of pregnant brown haystacks. The timing of fourth and final stage of the peanut harvest ultimately depended on the availability of a piece of machinery called a peanut thrasher or combine. These huge, privately owned machines completed the harvest by separating the plants into hay for the livestock and peanuts for people.

Peanut thrashing day was also harvest day for Mr. Jiggs and the other farm cats. As the haystacks were cleared, hundreds of field mice, their peanut palaces having been rudely taken away, would scamper for their very lives. Newsreel pictures Jubal and his father were seeing at the Saturday night movies would show the people in eastern Europe running like the mice in their peanut field as they fled from their Nazi attackers.

Jubal chose to spend the bulk of his spare time with Uncle Frank. The boy especially enjoyed being with the old man at the mule barn, where Uncle Frank spent most of his time. Of all the farm animals, the mules were Ruffin's favorites. Uncle Frank would tell the boy wonderful stories about the life of each one. Aunt Sarah's household and garden chores, however, often cut into their fishing, barnyard and storytelling time.

Aunt Sarah could be very blunt and bothersome at times. "If you goin' waste yoh time hangin' out wid yo Uncle Frank, den you'ze gone hafta hep him wid his work, and dat means tendin' de garden, feedin' de pigs and de chickens and hillin' dem sweet taters yonder, too ."

Harvesting and storing sweet potatoes was an especially time- consuming job. "Taters" had to be manually dug out of the ground with a hoe and transported to the end of the. garden row nearest the house. There Jubal stacked the sweet potatoes evenly onto alternating piles of pine straw and garden dirt. The dirt insulated the potatoes, and the pine straw would allowed the water to drain away. Properly "hilled" sweet potatoes could survive outdoors and above ground without either freezing or rotting during the long winter months.

Uncle Frank managed to get down on his knees, but sometimes he couldn't get up. One day when Aunt Sarah sent the poor man for sweet potatoes, Uncle Frank had to crawl all the way back to the house. After that, she assigned the chore of getting sweet potatoes from the hill to Jubal and herself. Because of his short arms, Jubal would often be in the hill to his armpits before he could reach the potatoes. Occasionally he would come out with a surprised mouse in hand, instead of a sweet potato. In the end, however, the process was worth the effort. Aunt Sarah could turn the world's ugliest sweet potato into Fallston's most beautiful and delicious pie.

Life on the farm had its chuckle--or good hearted laughter. One morning Uncle Frank accidentally let the calf get loose. The Scotts were eating breakfast when Aunt Sarah looked out the kitchen window and saw the calf helping herself to Aunt Sarah's vegetable garden. What the calf wasn't eating, she was destroying with her feet. To make matters worse, Uncle Frank was creating more havoc than the happy calf was. Mason, Aunt Sarah and Jubal rushed out to help. The calf became frightened and left the garden in a hurry, heading for the country road. "Run, Uncle Frank, run!" the boss yelled.

Uncle Frank reacted obediently by "running," only to be yelled at again. "Where in the world are you going, Uncle Frank? The calf is this way."

"Mister Mason, yo said run. Yo didn't say which a' way," came Uncle Frank's classic explanation.

Because of his bandy legs, Uncle Frank could not walk to the river and back in a week, much less an afternoon. But luckily, Chester, the farm's semi-retired mule that couldn't do much of anything else, continued to make that walk smartly. The old man and the old mule were inseparable friends around the barn. Uncle Frank often talked to Chester about his aches, pains and problems. Because of their positions of honorable lifetimes of service, Chester and Uncle Frank were in a class by themselves. Whether it was plowing the garden or pulling the cart, the two moved at the same pace. Chester seemed to know that he was alive because Uncle Frank was alive. Uncle Frank would come to the barn door and yell "Chester." And, Chester would usually be waiting on the opposite side. Uncle Frank would open the door and out would come the plodding old-timer. Chester would see fishing gear, go to the cart and back himself into the shaft and wait patiently to be harnessed.

For weeks Jubal held out hope that the locomotive explosion mystery was about to be solved. After all, he reasoned, the smartest people in the world were working on the case. As weeks became months the boy gradually began to give up. Then one night at bedtime, Mason confided to the boy that there were no new clues. Bob Dunbar was no closer to solving the case than at the beginning.

Jubal was so turned off by his father's news that he decided to give Uncle Frank a piece of his mind the next morning.

Before leaving for school, the boy found Uncle Frank at the mule barn and gave his prepared lecture. He concluded his salvos saying with ten-year-old conviction, "It's about time some people around here wised up!"

"Who is deze some people you'ze referrin' to, boy?"

"You for one, me for two. And Papa. And the sheriff. And Mrs. Brandon, that's who."

"And jus' whut is it dat we needs to wise up 'bout. Pray tell me."

"We've all been fiddling around, doing nothing about catching those bad guys. All of us must be just plain stupid. I'm tellin' you, there ain't ever gonna be no Mr. Scott and Mrs. Brandon riding off into no sunset nowhere around these parts unless somebody starts getting serious about solving this case. It's gonna take more than talkin, scheming' and writing to bogus watch companies. Somebody's gotta bait a trap if they want to catch a fox. You taught me that much, Uncle Frank. The way things are going around here, this case ain't never gonna get solved."

"Now you jus' lisen to me fer a minute, boy. If'n it won't fer yo papa's concern for yo life and mine, maybe dem men would be a' sittin' in jail right now."

"Our lives? What kind of lives have we got to save?"

"Look boy, hit's time for yo to git to school. So I ain't got time to explain everything. Ize grants yo hit would likely be easy to flush de man out if'n dat man thought dat you had dat watch of hisen. But de question is would dat man get yo befoe de police gets him? Believe me, boy, If'n yo pa knew how to catch dat man widout puttin' you and me in danger, he'd a dun dat long ago. Now you hush up dis foolishness and git on to yo schoolin'. We can talk 'bout dis later."

Fifteen minutes later, Jubal parted company with the black kids and was on his own for the second half-mile of his walk to school. The boy was feeling about as low as he thought possible, totally emerged in self-pity. He was thinking, "Well, there it is again. I'm the problem. I've always been the problem."

The boy left home as he had on every previous school morning this term. Hot weather had been with them right along with little or no break in sight. Jubal thought that he was properly dressed for the weather, but a cold front had moved through during the night, and now the weather was adding to the boy's misery. Luckily, however, the steady stiff cold breeze was now against his back. Jubal was wearing his usual short-sleeve shirt and short pants. He hunched himself into the smallest possible target, and as was his habit, was walking in the middle of the railroad track. Jubal's father had prescribed this as the safest place for him during that part of the walk. Suddenly, without warning the pulpwood train jumped into view and was bearing down on the boy. The surprise was punctuated, not by the familiar shriek of a steam whistle, but by the loudest horn the boy had ever heard. And he found himself face to face with the first diesel engine he had ever seen.

The strange monster was approaching the boy head-on at a pretty good clip. Jubal stood frozen in the middle of the track. The engineer decided he'd better give the boy another blast with his horn. That woke Jubal up, and he watched the train zip by from a safe distance. Two minutes later the gently swaying caboose had rounded the next bend in the looping track. The train went out of sight and sound, leaving an impression that remained with Jubal for a long, long time. The boy learned two things that he had not known previously. Uncle Frank was wrong; a locomotive can sneak up on a hearing person! More importantly, however, he knew without a doubt that the man in the fireman's seat of that locomotive was the same man who grabbed him on the night of the explosion.

Normally, the boy's brain would have stored a detailed image of the diesel locomotive, one which he could recall, describe and embellish at his leisure. It would, of course, have been an image that, at his earliest opportunity he would communicate grandly to Uncle Frank. The pair already had held many discussions about diesel engines. Although Jubal actually knew next to nothing about diesels, he'd attempted to impress Uncle Frank with the few key-words he'd picked up: efficiency, technology, power. Uncle Frank scoffed at the idea that any locomotive would ever be powerful enough to replace the mighty steam engine. "And, if'n dey evah is one, yo' ole Uncle Frank won't be heah to see hit."

Except for the double warning of its horn, however, the boy remembered next to nothing about that particular diesel. He rationalized that perhaps the locomotive was too close for him to study details. But most importantly, Jubal remembered the man in the fireman's window.

The two-way recognition between the man and boy was instantaneous. Once their eyes met they became mutually controlled robots, heads rotating involuntarily in unison, maintaining a continuous line-of-sight to the last second possible. It was impossible for Jubal to know, much less recall, the full range of emotions that passed between them in those unforgettable seconds. But one thing was obvious, information was being transmitted in both directions. Jubal remembered being terrified and yet keenly aware that the man in the locomotive was upset as well.

The two were like prize fighters, touching gloves, each wishing the other well, each knowing that only one of them could win. Fate had them locked in a struggle that neither wanted or chose. In that moment Jubal felt a surge of compassion for the man. He wanted things to be all right between them.

The train disappeared, and the boy was alone. It didn't take long after that for fear to overtake Jubal. He had completely forgotten the police whistle his father had given him. All he could think of was putting distance between him and that man. The boy made the trip home in record time and stumbled into the yard, yelling. "Papa, Aunt Sarah, Uncle Frank, HELP, HELP, HELP!"

Aunt Sarah met the boy on the back porch, and the boy fell into her arms. He was completely winded, with his sides ready to explode. The boy's legs could have taken him no further. Aunt Sarah held him. Jubal was trembling.

"Where's Papa?"

"He done gone to Centerville wid a load of 'bacca. He ain't gone be back heah afore night. What's wrong wid you, boy? Yo look like you just seen a ghost."

"It's worse than that. I just saw the man who grabbed me that night. He's over at Fallston right now, this very minute on the pulpwood train. I just saw him. He may be on the way to kill me right this minute."

Uncle Frank appeared, wanting to know what was wrong. Aunt Sarah held the boy tightly and the boy held her. When Jubal regained enough composure, he gave a fairly clear account of what he had just seen and experienced. Aunt Sarah's response was instantaneous.

"Jubal, you git to de phone dis minute and call Sheriff Bob, tell him we needs him or one of dem deputies o' hisn out heah as fast as dey can travel. Frank, you fetch me yo ole shotgun. Den, I wants you go yonder and find Brodus or one of the other men and send dem heah as fast as you can. If you don't find no man, den send some of de women."

As Uncle Frank was leaving he turned to Jubal and asked, "Jube, is yo' sho' dat was one of dem diesels? I sho' would love to see me one of dem things."

"Frank Ruffin, have you completely los yo mind? Dis ain't no time fo yo to be seein' nothing but somebody to hep us if'n dat man comes here."

"One thing's fur sho. Dat man ain't comin heah no time soon," Uncle Frank countered.

"Whut makes yo so sho bout dat?" Aunt Sarah asked, while shoving a shell into the barrel of the shotgun.

"Cause. If'n dat man is workin' on dat locomotive, he can't jus' run off and leave his job. If'n he done dat he'd leave a guilty trail as clar as a fox dat's dum enough to git hisself shot whilst he's in de hen house."

"Dat may-be so, but we ain't takin' no chances. If dat man knows whut Jubal knows, den he knows dat he's got to catch up wid you and Jubal afore de law catches up wid him. Now, ain't dat so, too?"

"Dat sho do makes sense, hit sho do. I'm a goin'. But, pray tell me how is dat pooh diesel gwine git all dat pulpwood back to Centerville?"

The past hour was the most frightening in the boy's life. He was thinking, "This is just like one of my old sick headaches. The things build and build for a long, long time, until something comes along and triggers them off in my head. At that point, I think I'm going to die and even wish that I could die. But there's nothing I can do but throw up, heave and suffer until I sleep. Then comes the good part: waking up. It is wonderful just to be alive again. Food is great again, life is great again. There is nothing I can't do."

That's the way Jubal was suddenly feeling about this business now. He became calm and confident, if not downright happy. Jubal Scott felt great. He told himself that he was now living the leading edge of the good part. Every sick headache brought him sympathy, favored status-- anything he wanted to eat or drink that could be reasonably found. He now sensed the beginning of the end of this railroad mess. The good part had started.

The way that Uncle Frank was handling the situation is what calmed the boy. As usual, the old man quickly grasped and addressed the situation with common sense as well as emotion. The old man was more awed by the diesel than Jubal had been by the man he'd seen riding in it. Uncle Frank may have been ninety years plus, but his keen perceptiveness, coolness and flair for life were alive and well. If Jubal or anyone else was not convinced of that fact by now, the next thing that Frank Ruffin did should convince everyone.

106

Chapter 19: The Alarm Goes Out

Aunt Sarah quickly reminded Jubal that nosy party-line listeners could be listening.

"Sheriff's office, Deputy Purvis speaking." At that precise moment the farm bell began to ring. Jubal looked out the window to see Uncle Frank pulling the bell rope with more vigor than anyone would have imagined possible for a man Frank Ruffin's age.

"Hello, hello, Sheriff's office, Deputy Purvis speaking. Who's calling? Can I help you?"

The boy needed to do two things at once, but he was more afraid that the deputy would hang up than he was that Uncle Frank would keep ringing the bell.

"Can I speak with Sheriff Dunbar?"

"The sheriff isn't here at the moment. He'll be here shortly. Can I help you."

"My name is Jubal Scott."

"Yes, Jubal, I know who you are. What can I do for you?" There was real concern in the voice on the other end.

"I'm at home right now. But on my way to school this morning, I saw that man again. Sheriff Duncan will know the man I'm talking about. He told me to let him know if I ever saw the man again."

"You stay right where you are, Jubal. One of us will be there in a few minutes. Understand?"

Jubal managed a "Yes," and he ran onto the side porch a second later.

"What in the world are you doing, Uncle Frank? Everybody within a mile will be here in no time." Jubal had to shout in order to have any chance of getting the attention of his well-meaning friend.

"Frank Ruffin, has you total loss yo mind?" Aunt Sarah was shouting at the same time from the back porch.

"Yaw'll said fo me to get some help heah in a hurry. Well, dat's whut Ize a'doin."

"Why did you let him ring the bell, Aunt Sarah?"

"I didn't let him do nuthin'. I come as quick as I hear dat bell," she answered.

"Why didn't you stop him? You musta heard him." she returned.

"I was on the phone, remember?"

Within five minutes people were were arriving at the farm yard by the dozens. Most were on foot, while others came in cars, carts, wagons, tractors, bicycles. Two were riding mules.

"What am I gonna tell these people?" the boy shouted to Aunt Sarah.

"I don't know, honey, but you better think'o sumpthin' awful quick like afore your Uncle Frank does dat job for you too."

Luckily Mason Scott, Sheriff Dunbar and Jubal had agreed on a story for just such an occasion. The boy could lie convincingly. He walked out and faced the crowd. Everyone was asking the same question: "What's wrong?"

The boy began, "It's OK, everything's all right now."

Jubal could see the relief on their concerned faces, but questions remained. This was yet another beautiful moment for the boy, all these good people coming to his rescue and no time to relish it.

Jubal, however, gave the performance of his life. "I've seen a man several times lately hanging out in the woods by the railroad track. On my way to school this morning, I saw that same man again. This morning the man started walking toward me. Then whenever I started running, he started running, too. I ran home as fast as I could. I've already called the sheriff. He's on his way here now. I'm sure the sheriff will find the man, and also find out what he's up to. After I told Uncle Frank and Aunt Sarah about the man, and while I was on the phone calling the sheriff, Uncle Frank decided to ring the bell. I'm sorry. I didn't mean to get the whole countryside excited."

A round of applause went up from the crowd. "Uncle Frank you did the right thing," someone yelled. The relieved crowd was milling around, apparently looking for someone to lead the posse. Another called, "You come on with us, Jubal. We'll find this guy for you."

As the vigilante was talking, the shrill wail of a siren and a cloud of dust were heading toward the scene. By the time Sheriff Dunbar arrived, the size of crowd had swelled to thirty.

The sheriff went directly to the boy. "What are all these people doing here? Are you all right Jube?"

"This is all Uncle Frank's doing." Jubal replied. "Aunt Sarah told him to get some help here fast. So, he goes out and rings the bell."

"Well, it looks like it worked," Sheriff Dunbar told the boy. And to the crowd he said, "Give me a minute to talk with Jubal, folks. I'll get back to you all as soon as I sort things out here."

They talked in the sheriff's car. Jubal told Bob Dunbar that he was positive that the man sitting in the left front seat of that diesel locomotive this very morning was the same man who grabbed and held him on the night of the explosion.

The sheriff wanted to know what Jubal had told the people. Jubal repeated what he'd told the first people who answered the bell.

"All right, folks," Sheriff Dunbar addressed the crowd. "Jubal here has already told most of you what happened. The boy spotted a strange man in the woods a couple of times recently and his father called the office to report it. On the way to school this morning, he saw a man he believes is that same man. That man made a move in Jubal's direction. Now all of you know what Jubal has gone through during the past few months. I think in his situation, everyone of us would have done the same. And Uncle Frank, bless his heart, was just doing his dead-level best to protect this boy.

"Aunt Sarah here sent Uncle Frank to get help in case the man was actually following Jubal. We can't blame Aunt Sarah and we sure can't blame Uncle Frank. He was merely making sure that nothing happened to Jubal. In fact I'm glad it happened this way. This actually turned out to be a real good drill. Uncle Frank and you folks have proven that the bell will bring help when and if someone needs it. It's good to know that all of you are willing to help. Jube's mystery man is probably some harmless drunk who probably got fired from one of those pulpwood crews. Those guys can look pretty scary even when they're sober. Thanks for your help. But you folks can go on home now. My deputy and I will have a look around."

Most of the volunteer militia were only too happy to be relieved. These drifted away quickly and quietly.   A few lingered, offering to help with the search. When these were politely refused and were out of earshot, the sheriff's attention quickly focused on the business at hand.

Jubal reiterated to the sheriff the details of his encounter with the man on the diesel engine.

"Are you positive that that man you saw this morning was the same man who grabbed you on the night of the explosion?" the sheriff asked, repeating a former question.

"Yes, sir." Jubal was becoming a little frustrated having to answer the same question several times Sheriff Dunbar turned quickly to Deputy Purvis. "Randy, you stay here and keep an eye on Jubal and Uncle Frank. Don't leave until I send someone out to relieve you."

And, moving faster than Jubal thought possible for a man his size, the sheriff was in his car and re-raising the clouds of dust that had barely had time to settle down. The sheriff's swift departure prompted Aunt Sarah to remark, "Dat man muss be in a Lawd almighty hurry. He ain't et one thing de whole time he wuz heah."

By mid-afternoon the sheriff and Mason Scott were back. The fact that they were arriving simultaneously suggested to Jubal that they had somehow joined forces in the manhunt for the man on the diesel. Meanwhile, the people at the house had arrived at a first-name basis with Deputy Randy Purvis. Uncle Frank and Jubal bombarded Randy with information about the case. While the deputy listened politely, Jubal finally realized that the deputy was thinking along other lines, namely the delicious aroma emanating from Aunt Sarah's famous cook stove.

Along with Aunt Sarah's marvelous free noon meal came the solution to at least one of the major mysteries that had been bothering Deputy Purvis. Randy Purvis now understood why the sheriff made so many visits to see the Scotts, and, more importantly, why these visits were so secretive and important that only the chief police officer of the county was qualified to handle them.

Jubal's expectations were running sky high, and he ran to meet his father and the sheriff. Jubal fully expected to be told that the man had been arrested, locked away in jail, and would never bother anyone again and that Melinda Brandon was coming to supper as part of the celebration.

"Did you catch him, Sheriff? Is he in jail now?" the boy yelled out to Sheriff Dunbar, who was holding a plain manila envelope in his hand. The sheriff's expression, however, was almost a blank. Jubal knew that something was wrong.

"Hold on a minute, Jube, here comes your pa," the sheriff answered. "We can save a lot of time and confusion by getting everyone together. When he gets here we'll have a talk, and everybody will know what's going on."

Even before they gathered in the living room the boy knew that he'd have to settle for something less than his expectations. He was young, but the boy knew from experience that fishermen and hunters can't resist telling their stories if the catching or killing has really been great. This bunch hadn't caught any fish.

As soon as they were settled in the parlor, Sheriff Dunbar began by asking, "For your pa's benefit, Jube, tell us what happened this morning on your way to school."

While Jubal was talking, Aunt Sarah and Uncle Frank nodded and mumbled their approval or agreement. Mason Scott looked directly at his son all the time the boy was talking, his eyes telling that he didn't believe him. When Jubal finished speaking, Mason turned his gaze back to Bob Duncan without a comment or question.

"I have here a photograph of the three men who were riding in that diesel locomotive this morning," the sheriff said. Aunt Sarah gasped as Bob Dunbar slid three large black and white prints from the manila envelope.

"Now, Jube, I want you to take a good look at these and let me know which one of these men is the one you saw on the train this morning."

Three seconds later, Jubal said, "None of these is the man I saw on the train this morning." Aunt Sarah summed up the sentiments of all when she cried, "Oh, Lawd."

Jubal was transformed from a hero to an object of pity in an instant. The adults in the room vented their disappointments in various ways. The two who affected Jubal most reacted in opposite ways. Aunt Sarah held out her arms, and he went to her. Jubal's father was threw up his hands up in the air in disgust.

"How could you do such a thing?" he stormed. "Do you have any idea how much time, money and energy you've wasted today? You've managed to make a fool of yourself and the rest of us, too You even managed to get the whole town of Fallston in an uproar. You get up to your room right this minute. You're getting a good licking for this escapade!"

"Naw, suh, Mister Scott, you ain't whuppin dis po child, not fo whut he done dis mawning you ain't."

Jubal's father took a menacing step toward Aunt Sarah and commanded firmly.

"Aunt Sarah, this is none of your business. Turn the boy loose."

Aunt Sarah tightened her grip on the boy. She was shaking with fear. Jubal was her cub, and the mama bear was neither ready nor willing to hand her cub over to be beaten.

"Dis po' chile wus white as a sheet when he come to me dis mawning. If'n he ain't seen dat man, he sho done seed his ghost right enough. Naw suh, if you gone whup him, you gone have to whup me, too."

"All right, Aunt Sarah, you win. Let the boy go to his room. I'm not going to whip him. But I don't want to ever hear you bring up the subject of this mysterious man again. Do you hear me, boy?"

"Yes, sir," Jubal managed weakly.

"From now on you're taking the school bus. You're not to go anywhere near that pulpwood train ever again. Is that clear?"

"Yes, sir, I understand."

Having challenged Jubal's father and won once, Aunt Sarah was eager to end the matter peaceably. She became a mother

112

hen and shooed her chick away from her lap. "Run along now, Jube honey. Go on up to yo room like yo pappy says."

As the boy was leaving the room, Mason Scott turned his attention to Sheriff Dunbar. "I'm sorry, Bob. I just don't know what in the world came over the boy."

"I'm sure Jube didn't mean any harm, Mason, and besides you don't hear Randy complaining. He got to eat one of Aunt Sarah's fabulous dinners, didn't you, Randy?"

Mason walked the two lawmen to their cars. Jubal watched from his room as the sheriff cars sped away, leaving him to decide if he was really crazy or being left to face a killer alone.

Chapter 20: The Luncheon Date

It finally occurred to Jubal that his shame, along with everything else associated with the explosion, was top secret and thus was known to only a few people. He had not, after all, become the disgraceful laughing stock of the entire world. Not yet, anyway. Things have a way of settling down after any storm. And, one of the worst storms of his young life had apparently blown over.

On the second Saturday of October 1941, his new Sunday school teacher, Miss Callie Parsons, called and invited Jubal to dinner after church the following day. In those days the Southern Baptist Sunday school year began on the first Sunday of each October.

Jubal figured that Miss Callie had invited everyone in his new class. But when Jubal asked several of his new classmates, none of them had been invited. Although Miss Callie Parsons was small in stature and well along in years she was not just your ordinary run-of-the-mill Sunday school teacher. Jubal was observant enough to know that Miss Callie Parsons was an important woman, and he was also sophisticated enough to wonder why she had been singled him out for such an honor.

Jubal reached her mansion at the appointed time and knocked. Knocking on Miss Callie's front door was like knocking on a tree. The door was so thick that Jubal couldn't even hear himself knocking. He stood for a while with nothing happening, just wondering what to try next. He had almost decided to look for another door when he spotted the doorbell button and pushed it . It was the first doorbell Jubal Scott had ever pushed. This time he heard bells ringing somewhere in the big house. In almost no time, a big black man wearing a black suit, white shirt and black string tie opened the door and looked down at the boy.

Jubal had heard that Miss Callie was rich, but until this visit to her house he hadn't thought much about it. He had heard, but wasn't impressed by the rumor, that she had two full-time servants to keep house for her. "So what," Jubal thought. "Papa and me have two house servants, don't we?" But when the boy washed up with gold-plated soap, and a maid served him sandwiches with the crust cut off and gave him a full bottle of Coca-Cola with a napkin wrapped around it, and he sat on a sofa so high that his feet didn't reach the floor, the boy knew that the Scotts and Parsons were not in the same league.

Sure enough, Jubal turned out to be the only guest. He soon learned that he had not been invited to dinner at all. This was, however, his first- ever business luncheon. They finished eating, and the maid took their dishes away. Then Miss Callie wasted no time in getting down to business.

"Jubal," she said softly, "I invited you here because I have something to tell you and something to ask you. The something that I have to tell you is something that I haven't told anyone else. The reason I haven't told this to anyone else is that what I am about to tell you may affect you more than anyone else. Let me start at the beginning. I was in New York City on a business trip the day before the locomotive explosion. I caught the train in New York and arrived in Centerville at one-thirty a.m. Edward, my butler-- you met Edward I believe, when you arrived for lunch a bit ago." She waited to make sure that she and the boy were communicating.

"If that was Edward in the black suit, the man that met me at the door, then yes, ma'am, I met him."

"Yes, that was Edward. Well, Edward met me at the train. There was a mixup with my luggage. That delayed us about an hour and a half. Just as we drove through Martin on the way home, we passed the pulpwood train. Well, this caught our attention. The railroad company had notified me that due to a huge increase in their workload of late, they may have to vary their pulpwood train schedule, but the railroad assured me that they would continue to pick up pulpwood three times each week. Even so, it was a shock to see the pulpwood train in the middle of the night like that."

"Yes, ma'am," the boy interrupted, "that's what Uncle Frank and I thought, too, as soon as we heard the whistle." They were communicating.

"While I was getting ready for bed," she continued, "I could hear the train making its way into town from the other side. I happened to look out my back bedroom window, in the direction of the barns where you and Uncle Frank were working, and I was surprised to see the lights of an automobile moving along Circle Drive. Car lights in the middle of the night on that road are very rare. The car was moving very slowly, as if the driver was searching for something. As I watched, the car turned off Circle Drive and moved slowly down the path toward your barns. It was soon behind the trees.

"I remember thinking, where can those people be going, there's nothing down there but a big ditch and the railroad track. Of course, I had no way of knowing that you and Uncle Frank were at the barns on the other side at the time. I only knew that the car must have been pretty close to the railroad tracks by the time I lost sight of it."

Jubal wasn't used to sandwiches with the crust cut off. He began to feel sick.

"I'm not asking you to say anything you're not supposed to say, Jubal. What I saw, and what I'm telling you now could mean absolutely nothing, or it could be very important. I saw a car go down that way. I am sure of that. Perhaps I should have said something to the sheriff or you or your father before now, but I didn't want to stir up trouble where there might not be any. Maybe it was just a coincidence that the car was there at that time, because I haven't heard anything to date to suggest that the explosion was anything but an accident. That is, I haven't heard anything specific."

Miss Callie was watching the boy closely as she talked. That "anything specific" probably meant that she was suspicious about the bell ringing business. Jubal recognized at least two clerks from Miss Callie's store in his yard on the morning of the Uncle Frank's bell ringing caper.

"I haven't been able to get that car out of my mind," she continued. "So I finally decided to tell you about it and see what your reaction might be. I know Uncle Frank doesn't see that well, so if anyone besides myself saw the car that I saw, that person would have to be you. It might not mean a thing. It could have been a couple on a date, or someone out for a ride in the country who simply got lost. But the fact remains that I have lived in this house all my life, and that car was the very first car I have ever seen go down that path after dark. For someone to choose that particular night and hour to go down that path makes me wonder. It is my duty to report unlawful behavior. I haven't heard of any unlawful act associated with the locomotive explosion. But to clear my own conscience I am going to tell Sheriff Dunbar what I saw, but I wanted to tell you first." She waited for Jubal to respond.

This was Jubal's Sunday school teacher. Was he supposed to lie to her? Jubal was afraid. He had barely survived the last battle with his father. The boy became very pale. It wouldn't be long before he needed to throw up. He had to get out of this house. When Jubal failed to respond, she continued.

"I went to bed. I was sleeping soundly when the locomotive exploded. The blast almost shook me out of bed. I ran to the window. I could see sparks high in the air for a few seconds. Then everything was dark again. That's when I saw the headlights of a car. It came out of the path and onto Circle Drive and headed west at high speed. The driver was obviously in a great hurry to leave Fallston. Now, that may not mean anything either. That explosion would have frightened anyone. On the other hand I can't help but wonder why the people in that car went down there at that particular time, and more importantly what they did do while they were there."

Finally the sick boy managed, "Suppose I did see a car, which I'm not saying I did, what's going to happen?"

"I honestly don't know the answer to that, Jubal. The last thing in the world I want to do is cause you trouble. But I wanted you to be the first to know what I saw that morning. If you think I should tell your father before I go to the sheriff, I'm more than willing to do that."

"Let me talk this over with my father first, please, ma'am," Jubal said softly, "before you tell the sheriff or anyone else, please. Papa gets awful upset when I do or say things without telling him first. And, if you don't mind, Miss Callie, I think I'd better be heading home now. I don't feel so good."

118

"Oh, I hope I haven't upset you too much."

"No, ma'am, it's just one of my old sick headaches working on me. I'll be all right in a little while."

"Can't I get you something, aspirin, a BC headache powder, or something?"

"No, ma'am, I don't think anything will help me. I just need a dark place where I can go to sleep."

"Well, if that's what you need, you can go to bed right here. I've got plenty of beds, and we can make it dark for you."

"Thank you, ma'am, but right now I need to get outdoors. I'll be all right."

"You certainly don't have to walk home in your condition. I'll call Edward. He'll take you home."

"Oh no, ma'am. I appreciate it, but it's best if I stay outdoors for awhile."

"If you think that's best, Jubal, then you run along now. When you're feeling better, talk this over with your father. I'll wait a day or two to hear from one of you before I say anything to Sheriff Duncan. But before you go, I have something for you and your father, something I brought back with me from New York."

She handed the boy a package, wrapped in brown paper. He could tell that the something was two books inside a tightly wrapped package. He could also tell that the books were the same size. Jubal took the package and left without bothering to thank Miss Callie for lunch or the presents. Miss Callie, however, knew that the boy was sick. Sick headaches had plagued the boy all his life. But they also have been used on several occasions to bail him out of some pretty tough situations. This time Jubal was genuinely sick.

The boy threw up several times on his way home. When he got home he tossed the package onto the floor of his room. Jubal didn't think of Miss Callie's gift again until he awoke around suppertime. As always, he was feeling great when he awoke. And as was his usual post-headache habit, the boy immediately broke for downstairs, hunting for food. These moments were the best of his life, the times when he was sharper and most alert. He spotted the discarded package, scooped it up and took it downstairs.   As he passed the parlor, he spotted his father reading the paper and listening to the radio.

"Here's a present Miss Callie sent to you and me. You can open it while I see if there's something like a chicken leg left on the stove. As soon as I get through eating, I need to talk to you about what Miss Callie Parsons told me while I was at her house this afternoon.   I'll be back in a few minutes."

The boy could be something else just after one of his headaches. He was thinking that his luncheon with Miss Parsons gave him not just an excuse, but an important reason to talk with his father about the explosion case again.

Chapter 21: The Journals

"Hey, Jube," Mason called out as he entered the kitchen door, "look what Miss Callie gave us!" Jubal could tell that his father was genuinely impressed. Mason Scott didn't get excited about many things.

While holding onto one of the books, Mason slid the other across the eating table in Jubal's direction. "Careful," he warned, "don't touch it with your greasy fingers."

The book looked expensive. Jubal was looking at the rich leather binding. "What is it? A Bible?" Jubal was expecting the words HOLY BIBLE, but even from an upside down angle, he could tell that this was not the title. He eased the book around with a clean finger and read the word JOURNAL.

"Look," Mason said, "I've got a journal too." He was holding the other book so that Jubal could read the title. The book Mason was holding was just like the boy's except for its color. The cover of the journal Mason held was dark green while Jubal's was royal blue.

"Why would she give us both copies of the same book? Can't we share?"

"This isn't a book you read. And it certainly isn't a book that you share. No, Jube, a journal is a very private book in which you write very private things."

"You mean there's no writing in these books now?"

"That's exactly what I mean. These are books for you and me to write about things we see and do everyday. It's like a diary."

"But diaries are for girls," Jubal protested.

"Well, I guess that's the reason these books are called journals. Journals must be for men. These are nice journals, too. We can swap if you like. You can have the green one if you want it. But keep in mind, young man, whichever one you choose, you choose for keeps. Once your name goes into a journal, it's your private property and your private business from then on. No one sees what you write without your permission. It's like those railroad workmen flags Mrs. Brandon told us about. No one can touch them except the person who owns them."

"I'll keep the blue one."

"We both need to write a thank-you notes to Miss Callie. These are nice presents. They'll hold a lot of memories. Now what were you saying about needing to talk? Something Miss Callie told you, I believe you said."

"Miss Callie saw the same car that I thought I saw that night of the explosion. She saw the car go down the path to the tracks about thirty minutes before the locomotive blew up. And she saw the car when it left, too."

Jubal could hear his father take in a deep breath. "She's going to tell the sheriff, but she said she wanted to tell me and you about it first."

"Why didn't she go to the sheriff right away? Did she happen to tell you that, too?"

"Well, in a way she did. She said that she kept waiting because nobody reported anything suspicious about the explosion. She thought that the people in the car might be lovers, or just plain lost, and she didn't see any need of stirring up trouble for people who didn't do any harm. At least, that's the way she explained it to me."

"Well then, why now?" Mason was getting more excited with each exchange.

"I can't tell you that, Papa. She just said her conscience was bothering her. She said she thought she needed to do the right thing and get it straight with me first. She figured that I was probably the only other person who could have seen the car. She also said that she didn't think that Uncle Frank's eyesight was good enough for him to have seen the car from that distance. That's about all she said."

"What did you tell her?"

"Nothing really, except that I would tell you what she told me, that's all. She said if she doesn't hear from us in a couple of days, she'll be calling us."

Jubal knew that his father was not listening, because both of them were talking at the same time. Jubal stopped talking and began to get the gist of what his father was saying, even though his father was obviously talking only to himself. "Something, something, some--thing, happened to make her change her mind about coming out with what she saw that night, and I think I know what that something was. Yes, that's it. It has to be Uncle Frank's bell ringing business.

"Listen, Jube," his father continues, "while you finish eating, I'm calling Bob Dunbar. Me and you are going to pay the sheriff a visit. And the sooner the better.

"What about the party-line business?"

"I don't think we need to worry about that problem any more. Unless I miss my guess, that woman is about to jump head over heels right into the middle of this crazy business with us."

It was dark by the time the pair met the sheriff in his office in Martin. Mason waited while Jubal told Bob Dunbar about his luncheon with Miss Callie Parsons, leaving out only the part about getting sick of her sandwiches. When Jubal finished, Mason said, "I guess you know what this means, don't you?"

"Well, for one thing it means we have a credible witness who saw something suspicious that night. That's about all I can think of at the moment."

"That's true enough, but that's not what I'm getting at. The fact that she saw that car that night might not mean a darn thing," Mason suggested.

"Well speak up, man, what is the big deal here? You didn't drive all the way over here just to tell me that her seeing the car doesn't mean anything did you?"

This was the opening Mason Scott was waiting for. "I'll bet my last dollar that Miss Callie Parsons knows a lot more than she's telling. Callie Parsons doesn't do anything without a reason. First, there was the car. Then the bell ringing. Now it's the journals. She wants Jube and me to start writing it all down. Do you see what I'm getting at?"

"Did she ask you anything about the man in the woods, or Uncle Frank ringing the bell, Jube?" the sheriff asked.

"No, sir," the boy answered.

The sheriff turned to Mason and asked, "If, like you say, she suspected something, why didn't she ask Jubal about the bell ringing, and the man in the woods?"

"I'm telling you the woman is too smart for that. And besides she didn't need to. Jubal got sick when she told him about the car going down to the track. Now I'm telling you, that woman's curiosity is up. That may not be a bad thing," Mason announced prophetically.

"Why do you say that?" the sheriff countered.

Mason Scott was on a roll now. Jubal hadn't seen his father this excited since the case began. "That woman has been waiting for a long time to get her hands on a real murder case-- ever since college days one of her friends told me recently. And lately, her friends say she seems to be obsessed by the idea."

"Well, the truth of the matter is, I need all the help I can get. This case is getting us all down and nowhere at the same time," the sheriff agreed.

"Why don't we give her a call right now?" Mason asked.

"I think I have a better idea," the sheriff said. "Why don't you have Mrs. Brandon come down for another visit? Now I know that nothing has happened on our end, but we did promise to keep in touch. Invite her to your church next Sunday. She'll stand out like a waterfall in the desert. Everybody in your church will know that the widow Brandon is in town, everybody, including our Miss Callie Parsons if you get my drift. Then, if what you say is true, Miss Parsons is going to want to have a talk with Melinda Brandon. Of course, there's a potential problem with this plan."

Mason Scott had already fallen for the idea, and he didn't want to hear about any potential problem. He also knew Bob Dunbar well enough to know what he was going to say, but he asked, "What's the problem?"

"Do you think we can survive working with two women detectives?"

Mason made the call from the sheriff's office. While the phone was ringing in Melinda's bedroom, Mason realized that it was almost eleven p.m.

Melinda Brandon was somewhat reluctant to answer. Lately there had been fewer crank calls.

"Hello?" by the tone of her voice she was asking, "Who is this?"

124

"Mrs. Brandon, this is Mason Scott. I'm sorry for calling you so late, but I'm here at the sheriff's office in Martin. We, that is Sheriff Dunbar and I, have decided that it is time for us to bring you up to date on the case. I'm hoping that you can visit us next Sunday. It would be great if you could get to Fallston Baptist Church in time for the eleven o'clock service. Aunt Sarah will have dinner for us after the service, and then after that we can talk. I know this is sudden. Do you need some time to think it over?"

"No, Mr. Mason, I don't need any time. I'll see you in church next Sunday." The phone went dead, and a pleasantly surprised Mason Scott said to the dead line, "Thank you very much, Mrs. Brandon, I'll be expecting you next Sunday morning at eleven o'clock sharp."

"Great," Bob Dunbar responded. "In the meantime we can either sit tight and wait for Miss Parsons to make her move or you can give her a call."

"I'm seeing that lady first thing tomorrow morning," Mason Scott answered.

"Come on, Jubal, let's go home. You've got school tomorrow."

Chapter 22: The Deal

The next morning before leaving for school Melinda Brandon prepared two lists. The first listed questions she intended to ask at her next meeting with the Scotts on Sunday. The second listed groceries she wanted delivered during the day. She picked up the phone and read the list to John Evans. "I will not be home until six or later this evening, so please have the boy put the meat and butter in the refrigerator," she told Evans.

Melinda's request was not unusual. Grocery boys in those days lived and worked in an open-door environment and were not only free, but expected to enter Centerville kitchens even if no one was at home. When no one was at home, the deliverer would be held accountable if the customer's order was not properly stored and refrigerated. Cash customers would leave money on the table. If the customer had only a twenty-dollar bill and the grocery order came to twelve fifty, the grocery boy would be given the correct change along with the customer's order. After phoning in her order, Melinda always left her list on the table. This way the boy would know if anything was missed.

At noon, Rex Evans, the grocer's nephew and grocery boy picked up Mrs. Brandon's order. "Is it all right if I go home to lunch after I deliver this to Mrs. Brandon's?"

"Oh, you run along home now, Rex. I've got to go right by Mrs. Brandon's on my way to the bank in a few minutes. I'll drop her order off on my way."

Most of the rural mansions in the Fallston area had been pillaged and burned during the Civil War. The farmhouse where the Scotts were living, however, was not destroyed. Its damage was caused by neglect and hard times during the years that followed, so-called years of reconstruction. The town of Fallston was completely spared by the Yankees when they marched through during the winter of 1864. A rich Yankee seaman-merchant by the name of Rawls took up residence in Fallston shortly before the war. Rawls, originally from Boston, is generally credited with the miracle of saving Fallston. And, with the Fallston farm being so close to town, perhaps Mr. Rawls should get the credit for saving that house as well.

Unfortunately, the locals also blamed Mr. Rawls for much of the havoc raised by roving Yankee troops during the war. The Yankees always seemed to know when the Confederate cannons guarding the railroad bridge north of Fallston were being manned. Probably, for reasons of health, Mr. Rawls quietly packed up and left Fallston soon after the war.

Fallston Baptist Church was the newest structure in around Fallston. The old ante-bellum wooden church building burned to the ground in the early 1930s. In spite of the Depression, the church was quickly rebuilt, almost entirely with Parsons money. Fallston was so near sea level that there were no basements. The top half of the new brick church consisted of a porch, two offices, entrance foyer and sanctuary. The ground floor housed the Sunday school classrooms, bathrooms, kitchen and fellowship hall. The congregation of Fallston Baptist Church took great pride in their new building. In spite of great differences in wealth and social standing, the church members appeared to be one warm, friendly family. Members knew each other so well that conversations between them were as predictable as the order of service on Sunday mornings. Visitors were rare. Beautiful, talented lady visitors were even rarer. Just as Sheriff Dunbar predicted, Fallston Baptist Church was not prepared for Melinda Brandon.

She arrived just as Sunday school broke up around 10:45. Jubal had hoped that he would be the one to welcome her. But Miss Callie kept her class longer than he liked. Jubal rounded the front corner of the church on the run, just in time to see his father opening Mrs. Brandon's car door. Melinda Brandon was wearing a bright green coat with big brass buttons. Her coat collar was made of genuine ermine fur. Her wide-brimmed white hat sported a bright red feather. She and Mason shook hands and talked for what seemed to the boy a very long time.

Jubal restrained himself to wait for them on the walkway out front. He was expecting at best a handshake. Instead, the widow gave the boy a genuine Baptist hug right there in front of dozens of people. She smelled, looked and felt wonderful all over again.

128

Following the hug, Melinda Brandon held Jubal's hand as they walked up the fourteen steps leading to the front porch. Earlier, the weather had been the point of much discussion. It was a cold, raw dreary morning, unusual for so early in November. But nobody was talking about the weather now. Inside, the narrow foyer led directly into the main sanctuary. The foyer was narrow because a pastor's study and the secretary's office were built on either side of the central hallway. Mason Scott was introducing his beautiful guest as he passed the curious regulars. Jubal had high hopes that his father would not be up to that job and pass it on to him. But Mason somehow rose to the occasion.

"This is Mrs. Brandon from Centerville. She's spending the day with Jubal and me." That was Mason's rehearsed announcement to each person they met. While his father seemed at ease, Jubal noticed a strain in his voice. He was sure Melinda's introduction was delivered exactly as his father had practiced it. There were handshakes and polite nods all around.

Mason helped Mrs. Brandon out of her coat and hung it carefully on a rack in one of two coat closets near the foyer. Except for the bright red feather in her hat and brown stockings, Mrs. Brandon was now wearing white from head to toe. The delay caused by her arrival meant that the Scotts' customary seats in the back row of the sanctuary were already filled and they would have to settle for the center of the church, much nearer the front than the Scotts' preferred. Several ushers vied for the job of seating them. After a pew was finally selected, Mason motioned for Melinda to enter ahead of him. This arrangement would have resulted in Jubal, Mason and Melinda in that order. But Mason's lovely guest would not cooperate. Instead, she motioned for the boy to enter first. She followed, thus seating herself between them. Chalk one up for Jubal.

The service opened with the singing of the Doxology. The power and sweetness of Melinda Brandon's voice virtually filled the place, sending chills over the boy's entire body. The acoustics in the sparsely furnished building were great. Anyone in the congregation not previously aware of her presence knew about her now. Those unfortunate enough to be seated further up front suffered the embarrassment of turning their heads. The organist stopped playing midway through and let Melinda's voice lead the congregation. Melinda's marvelous voice gave that worship service a genuine spiritual lift.

The boy rode with Melinda from the church to the farmhouse. It was nice having her to himself. Earlier, Jubal had a thousand things on his mind to tell her. Now that they were alone, none seemed worth saying.

Finally he managed, "You have a beautiful voice. I didn't know anyone could sing like that."

"Thank you Jubal, that's very sweet of you to say that. I enjoyed singing with your people. You have a very nice church. I'm very pleased that your father invited me." Then suddenly she changed the subject. "I understand from your father that there has been developments in the case. What's up?" The question was asked lightly, but the message was clear. The boy knew instantly that Melinda Brandon wasn't here on a mere social visit or to sing the Doxoloy for folks at Fallston Baptist.

Jubal didn't answer. He was afraid that he'd get in trouble for talking without first telling his father what he planned to say. He wanted desperately to tell her about seeing the man on the diesel. But his father had made it very clear that subject was closed. Suddenly the boy felt a great pity for his father. In Jubal's mind, his father simply didn't understand that Melinda Brandon was here for one reason and one reason only: to find out who killed her husband. In the boy's mind, his father was so blindly in love with Melinda Brandon that he couldn't see what she was up to. Mason Scott, however, was no fool. He knew even better than his son that the case was going nowhere. Jubal was right about the fact that his father was deeply in love with the widow Brandon. But that had not blinded Mason Scott to the facts. He, too, knew why Melinda Brandon was in Fallston. Mason Scott had a plan. And so did his son.

Jubal knew that the fact that Miss Callie Parsons had seen the car would do little more than reinforce what Melinda Brandon already knew. Jubal knew deep down that when a report no more meaningful than somebody seeing a car in the vicinity of the explosion that night reached Melinda Brandon's beautiful ears, that pretty lady would be out of the Scotts' miserable lives again. Melinda Brandon already knew that there was somebody messing around down there. This time she'd probably be gone forever he thought. The boy was on the verge of tears. As if reading his mind, Melinda reached over and took the boy's hand.

That did it. The boy's entire body and soul was nothing but a blob of Melinda Brandon putty now. He said, "I'll tell you something, but you'll have to promise me that you won't tell Papa that I told you. Is that a deal?" They were very near the lane to Jubal's house. She released his hand to make the turn into the lane. "Deal," she said and patted his hand, prompting him to go on.

"No one here believes me, but I saw the man who grabbed me. He was on the pulpwood train about ten days ago. I saw him and he saw me. He was on the diesel. It happened the very first day a diesel ever came to Fallston. It was him. I know it was him."

"Why doesn't your father believe you?" Mason pulled up beside them. She squeezed the boy's hand firmly and said, "OK, Jubal, this is just between you and me for now. We'll talk about it later in private." She let the boy's hand go just as Mason Scott opened the door on her side.

Chapter 23: The Lady Makes a Call

While his father was busy entertaining their guest, the boy slipped upstairs and changed out of his Sunday clothes. The boy knew that his father preoccupied as he was, had not missed him until he showed up at the dinner table dressed in overalls. The moment he saw what the boy had done, Jubal received his father's undivided attention. The boy's father crossed the room in less steps than the NBA referees call traveling today. Ordinarily Jubal would have been smacked, but Mason Scott managed to check himself without actually delivering a blow. Instead, the boy received an ugly dressing down. Jubal deliberately baited his father. His father took the bait and made a fool of himself in the bargain. So much for the effect of the Sunday sermon.

Otherwise, the noon meal was a complete success. Aunt Sarah, a culinary perfectionist, made everything just right. After the marvelous dinner, the boy was surprised to discover the parlor as cozy as the dining room had been. The Scotts' parlor was normally uninhabitable during the winter months. Until now the fireplace had been no match for the combination of high ceiling and drafty windows, doors and walls. But while Jubal was away at school that week, his father accomplished what looked like a miracle to his son. The crackling fire in the fireplace was now generating just the right amount of heat. The addition of new curtains, a fresh coat of paint, and several of Aunt Sarah's flowering plants gave the previously drab room a homey look and comfortable feeling.

Much of the after-dinner talk turned to the subject of Melinda Brandon's singing voice. Mason Scott and son were not the only ones impressed with the way she sang. They left the church in Melinda shock.

Neither were surprised to learn that Melinda Brandon was a music teacher in the public schools of Centerville. She downplayed her talent, saying that her singing voice was merely a God-given talent, a way God gave her to express the joy that He had placed in her heart. They talked about the war news, the weather, the price of tobacco--everything except the case. When widow Brandon could bear it no longer, she looked directly into Mason Scott's eyes and asked, "Has the sheriff made any significant progress toward finding the man who accosted Jubal on the night of the explosion?"

"In a word, nothing," Mason answered rather weakly.

"Nothing?" she repeated, disappointment audible in her response.

Jubal's father then went into a rather involved and stammering explanation about what he had found out about the watch business. While he provided plenty of wordy explanations, he provided no useful information. And in the end Mason sadly reported that his search had ended in an ocean of red tape.

Mason told them, "The watch Jubal took from the man came from a newly manufactured batch of watches which looks very similar to the watch I have been holding onto for years. A new batch of watches, including the one Jube took from the man on the night of the explosion, has recently been sold by the hundreds to railroad shopmen as Centerville. And even worse, hundreds of non-railroad people in and around Centerville have also purchased watches from this new batch as well. While the watch Jubal took is hard evidence that a man was on the scene that night, the chances of ever locating that man based upon the ownership of that watch is now highly unlikely. I'm sorry," Mason concluded, "but, unless something changes, I don't see that we are any nearer solving this case than we were the last time you were here."

The room suddenly seemed very cold. At least the dying fire gave Mason something to do besides relating bad news. While Mrs. Brandon stared blankly, he stoked the fire with the iron poker and shoved several small pieces of kindling wood atop the now smoldering fire. The room was so quiet that they could hear the fire begin to crackle and the sound of Mason brushing imaginary sawdust from his hands.

Finally, after a soundless eternity she stood and said, "I really need to be going. The meal was wonderful. Please tell

Aunt Sarah again that I enjoyed it very much. Could I have my coat now, please?"

Even in an ordinary situation Mason Scott usually found little to say. Now, he was totally mute. He wordlessly retrieved her coat and held it while she slipped quickly into it.

At the door, she turned and looked at them. Both sensed that she may be saying goodbye forever. Instead she asked, "Would you mind, Mr. Scott, if I borrow Jubal for a little while? Miss Parsons, a lady at your church phoned me earlier in the week and asked if I would stop by her house in Fallston on my way home. I promised that I would. Perhaps you'd be so kind as to allow Jubal to show me where she lives. I'll have him back home in an hour or so, I promise."

Jubal looked at his father, who was still speechless.

"Can I go, Pa?"

"May I go," Mrs. Brandon corrected.

The boy had read somewhere that big things sometimes turn on one single little word fitly spoken, or something close to that, but Jubal was not prepared for what happened next. As the boy and his guest were on their way out, the man who normally had few words to impart, made a request. "Look, Mrs. Brandon, would you please come back and sit down for a couple of minutes more. I have something to say that you may or may not be interested in. I want you to hear it now if you don't mind."

The temperature in the room had risen dramatically. She slipped out of her coat, laid it across an empty chair, and dutifully crossed over to the sofa and sat down beside the boy.

Mason Scott was very nervous. While the widow and Jubal waited, Mason Scott paced around the large room. He looked like a court-room lawyer now, searching for the exact moment, the moment of maximum impact before delivering his carefully prepared statement.

"Four years ago," he began calmly, "my wife died. Since then I have been without doubt the loneliest man in the whole world. Then one day a few weeks ago you showed up here in this yard and then in this room. From that moment, much of the loneliness has gone out of my life. And today, just now, something, I guess it must have been the voice of God, told me that I am no longer the loneliest person in this world." And looking Melinda Brandon straight in the eye he said calmly "You must be that loneliest person now."

Melinda Brandon began to sob. The boy touched her hand and she took it and squeezed it tightly. Meanwhile Mason Scott continued.

"I have spent these last four years of my life like Job in the Bible. I have been sitting in the ashes of my life wondering why God has chosen to punish me so. Now God has seen fit to give me a new reason to live. I don't intend to let this opportunity slip away from me. Lately I've wondered a lot about what to do with my life. Now I know. I'm leaving the farm. I'm going to get a job at the railroad shops in Centerville. I've looked into the labor situation there, and I have been told that I am qualified for a job there. I believe that one of those men at that railroad shops killed your husband. I'm going to find that man and see that he is brought to justice."

Melinda Brandon blew her nose and looked at Mason Scott, now standing a few feet away. She released the boy's hand and stood facing his father. They walked into each other's arms and hugged. Brother-and- sister-type hugging. But both were clearly reluctant to break their embrace.

Jubal was in total shock. He had never for a moment entertained the idea of leaving the farm. The end of the year was not far away. He knew that year end is when farm manager's contracts end. Until this moment he, too thought that he was willing to do anything for her, but moving to that sooty old town had not crossed his mind.

Jubal was wakened from his reverie by his father's still shaky voice. "Get your coat, son, and ride with Mrs. Brandon over to Miss Callie's house now. By the time you two get back, I'll see if Aunt Sarah can't round us up a little supper."

The atmosphere had completely changed now.

"I wonder why Miss Callie wants to see me?"

"She probably wants to know if she can recruit you for the Fallston Baptist choir," Jubal offered.

"Although that's a very good idea, I don't think that's what she wants," Mason countered.

136

Mason's tone was much lighter now. The man seemed completely at ease. The atmosphere was so relaxed that Jubal forgot about his father's orders not to discuss the case with anyone.

"Miss Callie saw that car go down by the tracks just before the explosion," the boy blurted. "That's probably what she wants to tell you."

"And she also knows that your husband was not the man who grabbed Jube on the night of the explosion," Mason added.

"You'll like Miss Callie. She's my Sunday school teacher. She's very nice and she's very, very rich."

"And, there's something else, too," Mason said. Jubal and his father were sending shots like tennis players, right and left and back and forth. "Jubal thinks he saw the man who grabbed him on the pulpwood train locomotive a couple of weeks ago."

Melinda looked at the boy and gave him a knowing nod.

The ball was in Jubal's court now and he volleyed, "But when I looked at a photograph of the locomotive crew, the man was not one of them."

"You see?" Mason said. "There's another reason I want to settle this thing. This case is driving us all crazy."

Melinda Brandon asked, "How did you get a picture of the crew?"

"Quite cleverly actually," Mason replied. "Bob Dunbar, you know the sheriff-- well, Bob called ahead to the newspaper office in Martin and asked if they would take a photograph of the crew for the newspaper. You see that locomotive was also the very first diesel engine to ever enter Green County. Its arrival was big news. So, you see, Bob gathered evidence without arousing anyone's suspicion. Pretty smart, eh?"

Mason did not receive the expected praise regarding the sheriff's cleverness. Instead, Melinda reacted with a question of her own. "Do you by any chance happen to have a copy of that particular paper? I'd like very much to see it."

"Why, yes, I have it up in my room," Mason answered.

While Mason went for the article, Melinda Brandon hugged the boy again. "This is turning out to be a wonderful day for me after all, Jubal. But I surely don't want your father to give up the

137

farm on my account. I hope I can convince him of that somehow. I must admit that his offering to give up the farm for my sake is the most wonderful thing that anyone has ever offered to do for me."

Mason returned with the Martin News. He had already opened the paper to the picture that had, thus far, amounted to Jubal's downfall. "Oh," she said, "I know one of those men. He goes to our church." She retrieved her pocketbook from the end table and pulled out an address book. "Do you mind if I use your phone?" she asked. "It's long distance, but I'll pay you for the call."

"Certainly. Go right ahead and don't worry about the long distance part. The phone is right there in the hallway just outside the door on your left."

They could hear her talking to the operator. Within seconds she was calling a man by his first name. In less that two minutes she was back with the news that there was someone else on the diesel that day, and she even had the man's name and general description.

"Yes, yes, Jubal, Rodney Peterson is a very large man," she said as she hugged the happy boy again.

Chapter 24: The Women Meet

Most Southern Baptists, unlike the majority of adults depicted in novels and movies, do not indulge in social drinking. However, Southern Baptists make up for alcohol abstinence with more than their share of social eating. As expected, Miss Callie had a spread ready for Jubal and Melinda Brandon. Fancy sandwiches, sodas with napkins wrapped around them, cookies and something Miriam called dip and crackers. Before that day was over, Melinda Brandon was overawed by the lady with the mansion. But it was far more than Miss Callie's big house or fancy food that impressed Melinda Brandon that day.

The two women hit if off from the second they met. Before leaving for Miss Callie's house, Mason Scott had given Melinda a brief profile of Fallston's leading lady.

"I'm sorry I missed meeting you at the church earlier this morning," Miss Callie began, "but I had nursery duty. And, as you well know, nursery duty always begins early and never ends early. Every parent who eventually made it to the nursery was raving about your beautiful voice. Singing aside, I feel as if I've known you for a long time, even before the locomotive explosion here in Fallston."

"I guess that you are referring to all the publicity following the tragedy last year at the railroad shops in Centerville."

"Yes, I followed that investigation very closely," Miss Callie answered.

"People everywhere, especially here in Fallston have been wonderful to me: Mr. Scott, Jubal, Uncle Frank Ruffin, Aunt Sarah and now, of course, yourself. I understand from Mr. Scott that you also saw the car that Jubal noticed on the night of the explosion."

"Yes, I did.   However, even if the people in that car had nothing to do with the blast, there is still reason for me to wonder what actually caused that explosion. As I mentioned earlier, I am familiar with your husband's involvement in the accident that resulted in a fatality at the Centerville Railroad Shops last year. I followed that case very closely. I never thought that a man with your husband's intelligence, long record of honesty, and service would remove a flag and then deliberately lie about it. Your husband and his crew were being paid by the hour. Why would they do a stupid thing like removing a worker's flag? It didn't make sense then, and it doesn't make sense now. No, I do not believe that your husband was culpable in the death of Harry Collins. I understand from reports I've read in the newspapers that you do not believe that the locomotive explosion at Fallston was an accident. Is that correct?"

"Yes, you are correct on both counts," Melinda answered with feeling.

"And, frankly neither do I."

Jubal could stand the suspense no longer. This mutual admiration was all well and good, but he had to ask a question, which he blurted out in a near-shouting decibel, "Aren't you going to tell Miss Callie about the big man on the diesel?"

"I'm sorry, Jubal. I guess I didn't realize how important that is to you, too," Melinda answered.

The widow and the boy began talking at the same time. Between them they finally managed to get the message across to Miss Callie that Jubal recently saw the man who grabbed him on the night of the explosion. That man was not Melinda Brandon's husband.

After that point was made, Melinda allowed Jubal to continue alone. The boy retold the story of his encounter with the man on the diesel. And without going into the painful situation that followed, he pointed to Melinda Brandon and announced proudly, "She even identified that man, and the police are looking for him right this very minute."

"How were you able to do this so quickly?" Miss Callie asked the widow.

The question was rightly directed at Melinda Brandon, but Jubal, who was on a roll now, was not about to give up the floor. The boy told the story up to the point when his father handed Melinda Brandon the Green County News. Finally the boy said, "I'll let Mrs. Brandon tell you what happened then."

When Melinda finished, Callie Parsons quipped, "Us women are not so dumb after all, are we Jubal? " and to Melinda

Brandon she asked, "What made you suspicious enough to ask to see the picture of the men on the locomotive?"

"Because," Melinda answered, "I guess I just trusted my instincts, that's all. And I trusted Jubal. After looking at those photos, I simply couldn't believe that Jubal could have been that mistaken."

Jubal added, "And the best part is I'm not crazy after all. The sheriff, Papa and everybody at my house thought that I had lost my mind."

"That is wonderful, Jubal, but I beg to differ with you about the best part. I think that the best part is that at last we have a suspect. A solid lead that shows promise of solving this mystery." Melinda was on the verge of tears, but for a change, tears of joy.

The time passed quickly at Miss Callie's. It was a happy time. But Jubal wisely laid off the sandwiches sans crust. He had not forgotten his last headache.

Melinda Brandon and Jubal reached the farm just as the sheriff arrived. He tipped his hat to Melinda as he slid a photograph out of an envelope and handed it to the boy.

"Is that the man you saw on the train, Jube?"

"Yes, sir, that's him."

"Have you caught him yet?" Jubal asked expectantly.

"No, but it's just a matter of time before we'll have him. The railroad company says he's out on the job right now. He'll probably be picked up before the day is out."

Chapter 25: The Reality Check

Deputy Purvis arrived at the farm just as they were finishing supper. Of course, it was the sheriff's duty to stay on until his relief showed up. The sheriff told the Scotts that one of his deputies would stay at the house around the clock until Rodney Peterson was picked up and questioned.

From what Randy Purvis had learned and was now telling, plus what the sheriff told them earlier, the Scotts began to get a fairly good idea of what Rodney Peterson was like. The fourth man on the diesel locomotive was a pipefitter working out of the railroad shops at Centerville. The "out" part was emphasized. According to the reports, Peterson was out of the shops more than in. Rodney Peterson was known in railroad parlance as a running repairman. Running repairmen traveled by train to wherever there was a problem. His job was to make temporary repairs that would otherwise take a piece of equipment or rolling stock out of service.

"Peterson was checking the diesel the day you saw him," the deputy said. "The diesel was brand new, and the pulpwood run to Fallston was its test run. Peterson was sent along to observe and make sure that the fuel injection system was working properly. Minor repairs to that system had been made at the round house in Centerville. Peterson went on the pulpwood run to make sure that those problems did not recur.

"Right now," the deputy continued, "Mr. Peterson is on the road somewhere. We haven't been able to locate him. Since he is authorized to do emergency work, sometimes at his own discretion, he is a very difficult man to keep track of. But we'll pick him up for questioning the minute he gets back to Centerville."

"You mean you're not going to arrest him?" Jubal complained.

"No," the sheriff said, "not for the time being. There's always the chance that you could be mistaken. And also there's also the chance that Mr. Peterson has an airtight alibi. And, of course, Mr. Peterson will be given a chance to explain what he was doing there, even if he admits to being at the scene of the explosion."

"Airtight alibi? What th' heck is that?" The boy was getting more upset as the conversation continued.

"An airtight alibi means that Peterson may be able to prove that he was someplace else at the time of the locomotive explosion. For instance, he may have witnesses. Witnesses are people who will swear that Peterson was someplace else other than at Fallston at the time of the explosion, that sort of thing. It might take us a while to build a case against him. Right now, all we have is your testimony that puts him at the scene of the explosion at the time of the explosion. Of course, we have Miss Parsons' testimony about the car. But she only saw the car, not the people in it. Her testimony will help collaborate yours, but so far there's no proof that Peterson or anyone else has actually committed a crime."

The sheriff used the Scott's phone to call his office. He was asking the person on the other end about a judge's order. Rodney Peterson was to be taken to the Centerville police station for questioning as soon as possible. The sheriff told his party that he was to be notified the moment Peterson arrives at the Centerville police station.

"How long will you be keeping a man here at the house?" Mason asked the sheriff as he was leaving.

"Just as long as it takes. Don't worry. We're going to take very good care of Jubal and Uncle Frank, too." And with that he was gone.

For the first time, Jubal began to be worry about what his father had been worried about all along. He was thinking, "Now, the police know who this man is. So what? Even if he is guilty of blowing up that locomotive, and killing those men, Rodney Peterson isn't about to tell the police about that. And even if I swear he was the man who grabbed me, it's my word against his. He can probably get a dozen cronies to say that he wasn't anywhere near here when the steam locomotive exploded. Who's going to take the word of a kid like me against somebody like Mr. Peterson? Furthermore, Peterson had a perfect right to be on the diesel when I saw him there a couple of weeks ago.

144

That only leaves the watch. And my father and the sheriff have already given up on that piece of junk."

That night Uncle Frank and Aunt Sarah were moved into an empty bedroom in the big house, and Deputy Gene Williams slept on the sofa in the living room. From his bed that night, the boy watched field, road and sky for any sign of movement. There was none. He closed his eyes and listened. Silence. His mind thus freed from distractions, he wondered where Rodney Peterson was right now. What was he thinking? Was this the end, or just the beginning? The boy relived that moment, the one when his hand broke free. He was remembering the smell of the whiskey. The strong arms. The watch. The diesel horn. The smell of new diesel oil.

The boy could not sleep. He made his way downstairs and found deputy Williams reading the paper and listening to music on the radio. "Oh, hi, Jubal. I thought you'd be asleep by now."

The clock read eleven ten. "Any word about Mr. Peterson?"

"No, not yet. The sheriff promised he'd give me a call if Peterson shows. I guess that means that he's still at work someplace. He probably went straight from one job to another. I'm told that his being away from home as much as a couple of days at a time is not unusual. Don't worry. He'll show up pretty soon."

"Or maybe Mr. Peterson got wind of the fact that the sheriff wants to see him and has taken off for good," Jubal suggested.

A vehicle drove into the yard, its lights flashing across the curtains. Jubal told the deputy that it was his father's pickup. He didn't want the deputy to think that it was Peterson and have him shoot up the place. Mason Scott had driven to Centerville, ostensively to see that Melinda Brandon reached home safely.

But when Jubal heard a man whistling, and the sound was coming toward the house, he almost got his father shot. He shook the deputy and said, "Somebody must have stolen Papa's truck and driven it here. My father never whistles." That caused the deputy to stand up and put his hand on his pistol, but it was Mason Scott. He bounded in the door asking, "What are you two doing up so late?"

145

"You must have good news," Jubal returned. "Mr. Peterson has confessed?"

"No, no, I haven't heard from Mr. Peterson. But he'll turn up soon," Mason answered cheerfully. Jubal thought, "My father is cheerful; that's a switch."

"I just hope he don't show up here tonight," was Jubal Scott's good- night speech and prayer as well.

Chapter 26: Bad News and Good

The boy awoke the next morning to both inside and outside noises. He ran to the window and looked out. There were several cars, including two marked with police insignia. From downstairs he could hear several men talking. Something big was up. He jumped into his clothes and ran downstairs. As the boy entered the room, a hush fell. Apparently, his appearance was the signal for them to shut up and drink their coffee. The silent treatment was not a good sign. Mason, who was seated at the table, stood and motioned for his son to follow.

The news was that Rodney Peterson had been questioned and released. Mr. Peterson claimed loudly and consistently that he was on an emergency repair job in Florence, South Carolina, at the time of the locomotive explosion in Fallston, North Carolina. The railroad company was quick to back up its employee's claim. Several witnesses were contacted by phone, and each confirmed Peterson's story. It just so happened that there had been a derailment near Florence just before the time of the explosion at Fallston.

"If it will make you feel any better, Jubal," his father added, "Sheriff Bob says that Rodney Peterson remembered seeing you that morning, and in fact recounted the eye-to-eye contact that he had with you, much the same way as you reported it to us. It turns out that Rodney Peterson has a boy about your age. Peterson says that you looked so cold and lonely that morning that he began to think about his own boy. He was thinking of how much he had neglected his own son, working long hours and constantly away from home. He said he sensed that you were reading his mind. In light of Mr. Peterson's size, age and the story he told to the sheriff, we understand why you thought that Mr. Peterson was the man who grabbed you."

"But he wasn't," Jubal moaned.

"No, son, he wasn't."

In less than an hour there were no cars left in the yard. Mason and his pickup were also gone. The boy had never been so lonely in all his life. Somehow, however, he managed to survive that miserable week.

As the days passed he knew that he was tempting fate. By all accounts he should have been having the worst headache of his life. Indeed, he felt a little worse each day as the long week slowly passed. For the first time in his life Jubal would have welcomed a headache. He desperately needed the sympathy. But his head couldn't or wouldn't get sick, that is, until the following Saturday afternoon. It was then that the headache struck the boy with all the forces that had been building for days. Aunt Sarah took one look at him and hustled the ashen-faced boy off to bed. She placed an extra slop bucket by his bed.

Neither sleep nor relief in any form came until there was nothing left for the boy to vomit. Still he continued to heave. He heaved until all the bile in his system finally passed through either his mouth or nostrils. Death would have been a relief.

Finally sometime, somehow the tortured boy dropped off to sleep. When he awoke on Sunday morning, Jubal looked out the window and saw his father driving away. He looked at his clock. It was almost time for Sunday school. Next he heard Brodus drive up in his old car. In a minute, as he watched, Aunt Sarah and Uncle Frank came out of the house and climbed in with Brodus, Dove and the girls. Those seven souls rumbled off toward Fallston. The Ruffins were going to church, too.

"Well, this is a fine how do you do," Jubal said to himself. "I guess they've left me here to die. It was ice cold in his room, so the boy didn't waste time with formal dress. He wrapped himself in his blanket and made his way to the kitchen. The fire had been banked and the stove was still warm. The boy's nose told him that food was near. And he knew where to look. He pulled down the metal door to the warming compartment above Aunt Sarah's wood stove. There he saw a most beautiful sight. A plate of home-made sausage, eggs and biscuits had been left for him. He also found a cold ginger ale left especially for him in the ice box. The boy was just finishing the best meal of his life when he heard a car drive into his yard. He ran to the dining room window and looked out. He did not recognize either the car or the two men inside it. But he could see that one of them was a very big man.

The boy had just survived the worst headache he'd ever had. This probably meant that he was sharper now than he'd ever been before in his life. It turned out that the boy would need all his wits to survive the next few minutes of his young life. Jubal knew instantly that he had only two choices. He could run to the phone and perhaps get off a call before they killed him, but that decision would not keep him alive; or he could use option two, Uncle Frank's plan. The bell ringing incident had been so successful that the old man had taken it upon himself to make it easier for anyone wanting or needing to repeat it. He tied a plow line to the bell cord and ran it into the dining room window. "If anybody shows up round heah whut looks like deys tendin' to hurt yo," the old man told the boy, "jus' run heah and pull dis line. Dat way you gone get hep in a hurry and scare dem off at de same time."

The shotgun Aunt Sarah loaded after the boy had seen Rodney Peterson on the diesel engine was still behind the dining room door, and upon the insistence of Uncle Frank was still loaded. As the men neared the porch, well within range of the shotgun, the boy poked the barrel through one of the panes, sending glass outward in several directions.

"Don't come any closer, or I'll shoot," he announced calmly.

The men stopped and froze. The smaller man on the left reached his hand into his coat pocket as the boy pulled back the hammer. It is amazing how sound carries when your life depends on it. The man pulled his hand out so the boy could see it.

"We're from the State Bureau of Investigation," the small one announced.

"What are you doing here?"

"We've come to see your father. Is he at home?"

Melinda Brandon who had arrived at Fallston Baptist Church for her second visit was now seated with Mason Scott. They were near the back of the sanctuary where the Scotts normally sat. Melinda, along with the Scotts, had been invited to Callie Parsons for lunch.

149

Callie Parsons approached Mason Scott hurriedly. She skipped the usual cordial preliminaries by asking, "Where is Jubal?"

"Why, he's at home," answered a startled Mason. "The boy's having another one of his bad headaches. I guess I should have gotten word to you."

"Who's at the house with Jubal now?"

"No one. Aunt Sarah and Uncle Frank were about to leave for church when I pulled out of the yard. He's all right. There's nothing any of us can do for him anyway. Those old headaches of his just have to run their course."

"You listen to me, man. You get yourself home this very minute. That son of yours could be in great danger at this very instant."

For another instant, however, Mason Scott simply stared at the woman giving commands. Mason Scott was not accustomed to being ordered around by any woman. But he didn't stare very long. Within the next minute, he and his pickup were well on their way home.

The two intruders at the farm were moving apart now, and the boy knew he didn't have much time. With his free hand, the boy jerked the rope as hard as he could and then gave it slack. The bell gave a loud peal. The men froze again, temporarily that is, until the bell rang again. The small man made a dash for the bell rope. Jubal pulled one of the two triggers, and the shotgun roared. As the boy was falling backward from the recoil, he noticed that the men had changed directions, both were now running toward their car.

While the big man got the car going, his passenger was waving a pistol in the general direction of the boy. The boy dropped to the floor, with glass all around him. As he lay on the floor looking down, he continued to yank and release the bell rope. He knew that he was safe for the moment. Uncle Frank had also taken the precaution of placing the two old dirt-filled wash tubs Aunt Sarah was using for growing flowers, just beneath the window sill. In the spring they'd be filled with pansies and periwinkles. It would take a cannon to penetrate the two feet of dirt, metal and wood that protected the boy. The shooting stopped, and the boy could tell that the car was speeding away.

The boy stood at the shattered window, shook a fist and yelled after them. "You should have waited, fellows. My father will be here any minute now."

And just as Jubal predicted, Mason Scott wheeled his pickup into the lane leading to the house only seconds after the men sped away. Mason Scott got only a glimpse of the car. He was much more concerned with what he might find when he reached the house.

There is only one way to get in and out of Fallston. Baptists, Pentecostals, black Methodists and white Methodists were soon occupying that way in totally integrated fashion. When two of the cars could not handle the excitement, momentarily blocking the road, they were quickly pushed aside and abandoned. The parade of automobiles and foot traffic kept coming. The boy ran into the yard and watched in awe as the line of people stretched as far as he could see. The boy shuddered to think how easily this could have been his funeral procession.

Within minutes the farmyard was literally filled with well-dressed happy people. Four congregations soon surrounded the boy as he stood in his underwear, mercifully covered with a blanket.

Once everyone saw and heard what had happened, and that the boy was not hurt, the crowd erupted in praises to the Lord. This was the first truly integrated religious service ever held in the South, and maybe in the nation as well. There was heartfelt and indiscriminate hugging and genuine joy on the faces of everyone. Someone took charge long enough to offer a prayer of thanksgiving. Following that, the combined choirs and congregations began singing spontaneously, "Amazing Grace" followed by "Blessed Assurance," and finally, "We Are Climbing Jacob's Ladder."

When Uncle Frank arrived, Jubal hugged and tearfully thanked the old man for saving his life. Uncle Frank had funny ideas, but no one was laughing about this one. The congregations finally began to segregate into their own groups. Soon the wail of sirens could be heard in the distance. Minutes

151

later, two deputy sheriffs were picking bullets out of the wall behind Aunt Sarah's stove. Jubal was asked to describe the men and their automobile. The boy told the sheriff that the men were dressed well enough to fit in with the church crowd. Both were wearing heavy coats, hats and dark glasses. One was a big man, about the size of the man who grabbed him. The other Jubal reported to be much smaller. The car they were driving was a fairly new Buick, light green, blue or brown. Jubal was color-blind and had trouble keeping colors straight.

"Maybe," he told Sheriff Dunbar, "after awhile, maybe I can think of something else, but right now, I'm not feeling very well."

They left some of the sheriff's men at the farmhouse to continue their investigation while the others went on to Miss Callie's for lunch or dinner, or whatever. On the way Melinda insisted that Jubal sit between herself and Mason.

"Better put Jube on the outside," Mason cautioned. "He's looking a little peaked. My boy can get sick awfully fast."

Melinda Brandon's car was a two-door, four-passenger car. She calmly folded down the passenger seat and said to Mason Scott, "You can sit back there. Then my hero can ride up here with me." She was soon cradling the boy's head against her shoulder. "You are one brave young man, Jubal Early Scott," she murmured sweetly. A voice from the rear said, "Well, what do you expect, like father, like son they say."

Before they reached Fallston, Melinda Brandon had to pull over, and Jubal threw up a large order of sausages, eggs and biscuits. Luckily his breakfast landed on the shoulder of the road instead of on Melinda's beautiful outfit. While the rest of her guests ate in the splendid formal dining room at Miss Callie's, the boy lay in a cool, dark distant room and wondered if he was going to live or die. He was thinking, "If this is what a hero's life is like, somebody else can have it."

That night Mason Scott wrote in his diary.

"Just to be on the safe side, Melinda is staying the night at Callie's. It was consensus at the meeting that she could possibly be in danger too. Fresh tire marks suggest that the two men who shot at Jube had earlier parked in the woods about a mile away.

152

Footprints leading to and from where the car was parked indicate that two men had earlier approached the house on foot. From a safe distance, probably using binoculars, they waited until they were satisfied that everyone else had left the house. Of course, Jubal, with some help from Uncle Frank messed up their plans."

That Sunday afternoon, while the boy slept at her house, Miss Callie promised her all-out commitment to the case. Mason Scott wrote later in his journal, "Miss Callie's promises that her role in the case is to be much more than lip service. From this day forward, Miss Callie Parsons promised Melinda, myself and Bob Dunbar that she intended to use every resource at her disposal to see that the men responsible for the murders and now attempted murder, be caught and brought to justice. She began by pledging to plan, finance and manage a safe haven for Uncle Frank, Aunt Sarah and the boy. Furthermore, she intends to hire the most prestigious private investigation company in the state to work on the case full time until it is solved. When asked why she was doing all of this, Miss Callie replied, "Oh, I guess you can say, so I can finally have the time of my life."

Melinda Brandon was waiting when Tom Evans opened the door to his grocery store. "Tom, you've got to help me," she told the surprised grocer. "I'm having a very special guest for supper tomorrow night."

"I'll be glad to help you if you invite me to come along," Tom responded. "What are we going to have?"

"I'm sorry to disappoint you, but this is a women-only thing. 'The' Miss Callie Parsons from Fallston is coming to my house for supper. Can you imagine that?"

"Hmm, this is big. To what do we owe this honor, pray tell." the grocer asked.

Suddenly Melinda became aware that she was about to share the happy news that the rich and famous were joining in the fight to find her husband's killer. Instead, she said to the curious grocer, "We're going to work on some special music for a revival they're planning for Miss Parsons' church down in Fallston."

Chapter 27: Uncle Frank Marks the Spot

For several days now Jubal sensed that his father had something very important to discuss with him. As the boy was doing homework at the kitchen table, his father asked a very odd question. "Do you by any chance remember hearing about the great Fallston Bank Robbery of 1934?"

"Yes, sir, that's the funniest story I've ever heard in my whole life."

"I'm sure a lot of people will agree with you. And maybe it is a funny story, but right now it isn't the funny part I want to talk about. Since you seem to know the story so well, you must remember that the robbers waited until all the guards were off duty. Then they robbed the bank when no guards were around. That's the part of the story that's worrying me now. We've got deputies stationed here at the house around the clock. We need to start thinking about what happens when the guards leave."

The great Fallston Robbery was funny. Until the locomotive exploded in Fallston, it was the one story about Fallston that practically everyone in the state east of Raleigh knew about. The robbery took place in the summer of 1934. The town marshal and lone lawman of Fallston at the time, received an anonymous tip that a famous bandit was planning to rob the Fallston Bank on a given night. On the strength of this tip, Marshal John Ayers mobilized the entire citizenry of Fallston and the surrounding area. Not since the Civil War had anything like this taken place in the otherwise peaceful town. There were guns everywhere: rooftops, trees and any place where people and guns could be hidden and aimed in the general direction of the bank. The guards, mostly farmers, had been up since daylight. Sometime after midnight, many hours after their usual bedtimes, the minutemen of Fallston began to get tired and were falling asleep en masse.

One particular weary, sleepy watchman was leaning back in a straight back chair that was leaning against a concrete wall. The man was inside the screened-in porch at the gas station across from the bank. That meant that there were not even enough mosquitos to keep him awake. Suddenly the chair slipped from under the exhausted sleeper and he crashed to the concrete floor. His rigid cane back chair and rifle leaning against it smacked the floor, making sounds like those of rapid gunfire.

The bank and the surrounding area were soon under an intense barrage of small arms fire. Once the gunsmoke settled, everybody decided it was time to go home. The very next night, bandits came and made off with the safe without drawing a shot. The kindest thing written about that fiasco was printed on a sign and posted under a bullet hole in the drug store window: The inscription read simply, "John Ayers' Hole."

"You say you remember the story?"

"Yes, sir, it was really funny."

"Funny or not, do you see what I'm getting at?"

"No, sir, not really."

Mason Scott knew his son was thinking about the Ayers sign. But Mason Scott was not in the mood for jokes. "The point I'm trying to get through your thick head, son, is this: Sheriff Dunbar's deputies will not be able to stay here indefinitely. The county can't afford it."

"So? I guess that means that we'll have to be ready for those guys if they show up here again."

"Oh no, son, that's not what it means at all. It means that when your protection leaves, then you and Uncle Frank are going to have to go somewhere where you two will be safe until we catch those guys."

"I could go and stay with Mrs. Brandon." The boy suggested candidly.

"I agree with your taste, but I don't think that would be a safe place for you or Mrs. Brandon."

"Yes, sir, I guess you're right about that."

"Nothing is going to happen right away. The sheriff hasn't said anything to me about taking his men away. I just want you to know that there's a chance that you and Uncle Frank will eventually have to go away someplace and I wanted you to have some time to think about it."

"Thank you for talking to me about it. Can, er, I mean may I tell Uncle Frank that we might have to go away someplace?"

"Not just yet. Maybe we'll get a break in the case soon. I don't see any reason to alarm the old-timer just yet. This has been Uncle Frank's home since the day he was born. I don't know how well he'll take the news."

The boy didn't take Papa's talk seriously until one morning when he was looking out his bedroom window, there wasn't a car in sight. That caught the boy's attention. Remembering the last time he was left at home alone, Jubal rushed downstairs and was relieved to see Randy Purvis at the dining room table.

"Hey, Randy, where's your car?"

"Oh, I put it under the barn shelter. I just thought it would be best if certain people thought that there were no police around."

A large map was now covering more than half the Scotts' eating table. "See?" Purvis said. "Here is your house right here." He was pointing with a table knife. It was a map of the area within a radius of about three miles of Fallston farm with the Scotts' farmhouse in the center. Jubal guessed correctly that the deputy didn't realize that the boy would know more about the map than he did.

Randy continued, "Over there is the town, and yonder is the river. We have people watching here and here and there, everywhere you see the big X's. If those people try to get in here we'll be ready for them."

Uncle Frank entered the kitchen as the map tour began.

"'Peers to me dat yo got yo X's in de wrong place," Uncle Frank offered.

"Why do you say that, Uncle Frank?" Jubal asked.

"Cause, if I wuz dem men, I'd come in yonder, by de river," he answered.

"What makes you think that, Uncle Frank?" the deputy asked, more out of respect than curiosity.

"Cause, dat's whut dem Yankees done. Dey didn't mess wid no roads. Is dat Yankee cabin on dat map of yourn?"

"What cabin?" Purvis asked.

157

"De one whut dem men who owns dis place use to stay in when deh comes heah huntin' and fishin'."

"Yeah, there it is right there," Jubal pointed out.

"Well dat's whar I'd hab my X's. Dem men might be down deah in dat cabin right now fur as all us knows. De owners sent word dat deys comin' down heah at de end of dis month, right after Thanksgivin'. I heard Brodus say dat him and Thad wuz thinkin' 'bout goin' down deah sometime today to clean de place and get it ready fur dem. Dem two's probably down deah right dis minute."

Just then they heard a woman screaming. The voice was coming from the direction of the river. They hurried onto the porch to discover Thad Walker's wife Liza toward them. "Help, help, somebody come quick." The woman was out of breath and appeared to be near collapse. "There's two white men with guns down by the cabin. Hurry, Thad and Mr. Brodus might get killed."

Chapter 28: A Close Encounter

"Did you get a good look at these men?" Randy asked the woman.

"No, sir, I hardly saw them at all. All I'm going by is what Thad said. He told me they's two white men."

"Where are these two white men now?"

"I hope and pray that they're gone on away from here. I heard a boat motor start up when I was on the way up here."

A huffing and puffing Uncle Frank joined them. Deputy Purvis said to Liza, "Go back to the house with Uncle Frank. Get on the phone and tell the Fallston operator to call the sheriff's department emergency number and she'll put you on the phone with our command post. Tell whoever answers what you just told us. Let them know that Jube and I are on our way to the cabin. Have them send someone to the house to stay with Uncle Frank. When they get there you and Uncle Frank can ride with them to the cabin and show them the way."

Jubal thought Randy was giving Liza more than she could handle. But she answered with a curt, "Yes, sir, I'll do that right away. Come on, Mister Frank."

"Is Brodus and Thad all right? Dat's all I wants to know" the old man was saying as the deputy and Jubal were about to leave.

"Yes, sir, Mister Frank, they're safe in the cabin. Thank the Lord they carried their shotguns with them. Yes, sir, they're all right, don't you worry," Liza answered.

"Everything is fine Uncle Frank. You go with Liza. Liza, you get on that phone the minute you get to the house. Jube, you come with me," the deputy ordered.

The two ran to the tractor shelter and jumped into the sheriff's car. Soon familiar scenes were flashing by at a rate that Jubal had never experienced before. The road was a little wider than a footpath, and at high speed in a swaying vehicle, it was like going through a dry car wash. The top of the boy's head hit the car roof several time during the ride. Randy turned on his siren to let Thad and Brodus know that friendly forces were on the way. Jubal figured that Boots and Thad had carried along their own guns so they could get in a little hunting.

Thad waved to them from the doorway. Randy went to the trunk of the cruiser and grabbed his rifle. The deputy ordered Jubal to stay in the car.

Moments later Randy motioned for Jubal to join them on the cabin porch. As Brodus explained what had happened, the deputy took notes. Brodus and Thad had taken their shotguns along because of the meeting that had taken place at the Scotts' house. That meeting took place after Jubal had gone to bed. Everyone on the farm was warned to be on the lookout for two white men who had attempted to kill Jubal. Everyone living on the farm was given a general description of the men and warned that these men were armed and dangerous.

Brodus began "When we first heard a boat motor nearby on the river, we thought nothing of it. Boats on the river are not unusual on any day when the weather is good like today. As the three of us were cleaning the cabin and writing down things we need to buy, Thad noticed two strange white men coming toward the cabin from the direction of the river. One was a little man and the other one big as the sheriff. The minute Thad spotted the men, he tells Liza to get out by the back door and get the deputy here as quick as she can. Thad watched Liza out the back window till she disappeared into the woods while I watched the men coming straight on towards the cabin from the front window.

"We could see that the men were carrying rifles. Neither one of us had shells in our shotguns. So we stayed inside out of sight and loaded up. We stayed inside till they got close enough so that our shotguns would have an advantage over their rifles. As soon as they got close enough we stepped onto the porch." Brodus interrupted his story by asking Thad, "Am I right so far?"

"You didn't tell the deputy that you made me bring my gun, and I was mighty glad of that about that time."

"What happened next?" The deputy prompted. He wanted more information without delay.

With Thad nodding in agreement, Brodus told about his conversation with the smaller man. According to Brodus, the smaller one did all the talking, a fact consistent with Jubal's previous encounter.

"What do you men want here?" Brodus asked the men.

"Is this the Kelly Cabin?" the smaller man wanted to know.

"No, sir. There ain't no Kelly Cabin around here that I know about."

"Well, we must be lost. Do you think it's all right if we hunt around here? We were told that it would be all right."

"No, sir. Like I say, you must be real lost. In the first place, this land is private owned and posted. In the second place, we've been expecting trouble. The police are looking everywhere in these parts for two white men with rifles. They told us one of these men is big and one of dem is little, just like you two. If I was you, mister, I wouldn't want to be lost nowhere around these parts, leastwise not today.

"That message must have done the trick. Them men turned their tails and headed for their boats awful quick. That little man who loved to talk so much, he didn't say one word."

"Damn," the deputy murmured, "that was probably those killers all right. I guess they're miles from here by now. Mind you, I'm not faulting you guys for letting them get away. You did exactly the right thing. We don't want anybody else getting killed if we can help it. Did you guys get a good look at them?"

"No, sir. Not if you mean like me and Thad would recognize them again if we saw them. No, sir, we didn't. They was both wearing sun- glasses, and they had on heavy hunting jackets. They had their hunting caps pulled way down over their eyes. Lucky for us the sun was right in their faces. It them men were the killers, I think the sun in their eyes is what kept them from shooting it out with us. With them high-powered rifles they had, they could stayed where they wuz and picked us off. I don't think they could exactly tell what kind of guns we had because of the bright sun in their eyes until they were right up on us."

"How far away would you say?"

"Somewhere bout fifteen, maybe twenty yards. What do you say, Thad?"

"About that," Thad agreed.

161

"So they got back in their boat and left. Which way did they go?"

"Down the river, towards the old battleground."

From his car radio Deputy Purvis called for a guard to be sent immediately to the site of the old fort. At the command post, Sheriff Dunbar ordered Deputy Gene Williams, "Get to the old fort as quick as you can. Watch for two white men traveling downstream in a small boat with an outboard motor." Probably not since the War Between the States had orders like those been issued.

Within the hour the center of activity shifted back to the Scotts' farmhouse. The Scotts' home became the temporary headquarters of Green County Sheriff's Department. People driving past the farmhouse would stop and gawk at the yard filled with police cars.

In his duty log, Deputy Gene Williams wrote, "Once I reached the top of the cliff, I spotted a boat containing two white men. They were passing directly beneath me. There were no other boats in my line of sight at the time. The boat I was watching was moving pretty fast. I could tell by the sound of their engine that they were probably running at full throttle. After their boat passed the bend of the river, they must have realized that no one upriver could see them now. I heard their engine throttle down. Since they were slowing down, I figured that they might be looking for some other spot to come ashore. That's why I stayed at my lookout. By staying at my post, I could have fired my revolver and signal a pursuit boat if one happened to come along. And, by staying, if the men did leave the river at some point, I could see that too. Of course no pursuit boats came and their boat didn't stop for as long as I could see them."

The forty-foot clay wall upon which Fort Rising was built during the Civil War is admittedly puny compared with the majestic cliffs out west. But to those living in the flatlands of eastern North Carolina, Fort Rising cliff was quite remarkable. At one time, maybe eons ago, the west bank of the Roanoke for several miles on either side of Fallston was probably lined with cliffs. Except for the cliffs here at Fort Rising only shadows of

162

those clay walls remain today. Locals now call what's left of the these cliffs Roanoke River low grounds. For long stretches along the river, and over eons of time, the river has eaten away at the cliffs until only Fort Rising, the river port at Fallston, and the low grounds remain. In many spots, the Roanoke low grounds have eaten mile-wide swaths. Here, underground streams, sinkholes and gullies have formed a natural border between the farmland and low ground's wilderness. Except for a few fearless bootleggers, little human use is made of the low grounds during cotton mouth moccasin season. In addition to the snakes, the area teemed with fish, deer, fox, wild turkey, ducks, geese and smaller game. In the fall and winter the low grounds became a paradise for hunters and fishermen.

Later that night, Mason Scott wrote in his journal. "Deputy Williams got to Fort Rising just in time to spot the men in their boat. Then came the moment of indecision on the deputy's part upon which the rest of this case may well depend. Deputy Williams could have left his post, gone below and used his car radio to report their location and heading. That round trip would have taken the deputy about ten minutes. Or, as he ultimately decided, Williams could stay at his post and continue to watch the two men head downstream until they were out of his sight. At the speed the boat was traveling, this would take about five minutes. I would have done exactly what the deputy did, except I would have stayed for a very different reason.

"Gene Williams was in the very spot where Belle and I went whenever we wanted to be alone. The happiest moments of my life were spent on the lookout at Fort Rising. I still go there as often as I can. Although I go there alone now, the place makes me realize that a part of that oneness we once shared can never be lost."

Jubal also wrote about Deputy Williams' experience at the fort that day. Jubal's entry reflected the fact that he'd spent the remainder of his afternoon listening to young Deputy Williams talk off the record about the incident. Jubal wrote, "While he was sitting up there on that hill, Deputy Williams felt like he was one of them old Confederate soldiers watching Yankees

163

sneaking down the Roanoke.   Sitting there listening to the deputy talking about all those ghosts gave me goose bumps."

Maybe a cellular phone at that crucial moment might have brought the case to a hasty end. Technology was changing the world, but not quite fast enough to solve that case that day. Again, maybe not. Perhaps those men weren't the killers at all. Maybe they were just a couple of lost hunters looking for a place called Kelly's Cabin where they had been told that they could hunt.

The aftermath of this incident made both of the Scotts think seriously about Mason's worry concerning the county's protection limits. There were simply too many X's on Randy's map. And these did not even include the cabin at the river until now. The county could not keep up this level of protection indefinitely. Even the ten-year-old boy believed that now.

Chapter 29: The Philadelphia Story

Jubal had matured during the past few months. He now thought that he could handle most anything. But he was not prepared for the news his father now shared with him.

"It's just for a short while, son. Aunt Sarah and Uncle Frank are going with you. Miss Callie has rented a nice apartment for the three of you. You'll be far enough away from here that nobody will know who you are or where you came from. Emily Clark is also going with the three of you. She'll be there so that you can keep up with your schoolwork. Emily has already made those arrangements with your teacher. You'll be living with Aunt Sarah and Uncle Frank, just like you're doing here. And I'm sure you'll get along fine with Emily. You know how nice she is."

For the first time in the boy's memory, his father seemed to be pleading with him. A pleading father did not set well with the boy. Jubal would rather have his misery straight, no sugar, no cream. He would have preferred that his father had said, "Young man, you're going and that's all there is to it."

Miss Callie's store van showed up in the Scotts' yard late that very night. Suitcases had been packed. When they left the farm, the sheriff's deputy who was on duty at the house rode with them in the van. Jubal was told that the sheriff himself would follow them until he was sure that they weren't being followed.

The van traveled until daylight. The women had fashioned the boy a comfortable pallet on the floor of the van, where he slept soundly until sunup. The stops, starts and clatter of big city traffic finally awakened him. For Emily Clark, this venture was a homecoming of sorts. Early in the Depression years, her family had moved from Martin to Philadelphia. Emily's father couldn't find work in North Carolina and finally, when a relative found Sam Clark a job in Philadelphia, the job was an offer the desperate man couldn't refuse. While the rest of her family moved to Philadelphia, Emily, who had almost finished her first year at the East Carolina Teachers College, stayed on in Greenville, North Carolina.

At the end of her first year of college, Emily was offered a teaching job in the elementary school at Fallston. In those days teachers were paid according to the years behind their certification. The state of North Carolina was only too happy to hire teachers with one-year certificates.

The young school teacher joined Fallston Baptist Church and was soon teaching Sunday school as well as singing in the church choir. Miss Callie recognized that the industrious young woman had potential that would fit into her plans. After teaching for one year at Fallston, Emily was hired as Miss Parsons' personal secretary. Miss Callie's long range-plan was to train the young woman to take over the operation of the store when she decided to slow down or step down. The loan of Emily Clark was a big sacrifice for Callie Parsons, but the answer to a prayer often comes C.O.D. rather than F.O.B.

The van stopped on a crowded street in Philadelphia, their destination. There was no front yard. No trees. Nothing to make the trio think that this was a place where people live. The row houses and apartments reminded them more of beehives than people houses.

Miss Callie's man helped with the luggage. Now, the boy fully awake, began to study his surroundings in earnest. He soon found himself in a long hallway with many doors. From one of these, several people ran out to greet them. It turned out that the furnished apartment Miss Callie had rented for the Scotts was across the hallway from the one being rented by Emily Clark's family.

Their new home was an apartment on the top floor of a six-story building. Thankfully the building had an elevator; otherwise, Uncle Frank would have been in big trouble. As his father has predicted, the place wasn't bad at all. And it came with everything they could have wished for. Comparatively, it was much more comfortable than their house on the farm. The view from the boy's bedroom window demonstrated both the good and bad of his current situation. Like the Roanoke of Uncle Frank's stories, the nearby Schuykill River was teeming with activity. And like the Roanoke, the Schuykill represented a very

166

clear dividing line. That comparison ended at the words "dividing line."

The Roanoke had fertile farmland on one side and spongy swampland, fit only for pulpwood on the other. Every square inch of land on the boy's side of the river at Philadelphia was covered with buildings, paved streets, cluttered alleys, traffic, soot and noise of every kind. Across the river he could see stretches of open spaces, punctuated with trees, parks, playgrounds and other signs of the good life.

The boy's new home was very near the open spaces, but yet very isolated from them. He stood at the window. and pointing across the nearby river he said, "Look, Uncle Frank, our house here is just the opposite from home. At home we lived on the good side of the river and looked at the swamp. Here we live in the swamp and look over at the good side."

The four displaced persons soon became lonely, sad and homesick. Of course, Jubal shared his feelings openly with Uncle Frank and Aunt Sarah. But now neither was able to help. If anything, the old couple were lonelier, sadder and more homesick than the boy. Days now seemed more like weeks and weeks like months. Uncle Frank coped by sleeping most of the time, and poor Aunt Sarah hardly slept at all. All began to wonder if they would ever see home again. They had been sent to Pennsylvania to die of loneliness and old age.

But Emily Clark and her family had no intentions of letting the three die on their hands. They began treating the homesick threesome with lavish doses of transplanted Southern hospitality. They took the trio on more day trips than there were days. They toured a few of the famous sites and more than a few of the infamous ones. They went to Independence Hall, City Hall, Horticultural Hall, Congress Hall and the pool hall. They visited the Liberty Bell, a museum, an aquarium, a zoological garden, a harbor filled with sea-going ships, and more and bigger department stores than the Fallston three imagined to be in existence. But most of their surprises came from conversations with the street bums who lived all around them.

Many of the street bums they met and talked with had a well-rounded grasp of the city's history. Their knowledge came

167

equally from street lore and the city library system, places where the homeless of Philadelphia apparently spent equal time.

America entered the war while they were in Philadelphia. In one way the start of the war added to their homesickness; in other ways it helped. As aliens, they realized that far more people than themselves were being separated from their families and facing far greater dangers as well.

Then on December 12, 1941, a month into their Yankee invasion, a letter came from Melinda Brandon. Miss Callie, it turned out, had exerted the full force of her influence upon the railroad. The railroad had now agreed to take photographs of all the shopmen on Bob Dunbar's list of suspects. These pictures would be forwarded to Jubal very soon. Even this, however, was depressing news. It meant the police were still counting on Jubal to identify the man.

"Haven't I messed up once?" Jubal moaned. "I don't have a clue what that man's face looked like. Doesn't Miss Callie and Bob Dunbar know that it was so dark out there that I never got a look at the man's ugly face?"

"How do you know dat de man was ugly?" Uncle Frank wanted to know.

"The same way you knew how to get me out of that watch business."

The boy was determined to take his frustration out on somebody, and since they were sent to Philadelphia that somebody was Uncle Frank.

"Now," Jubal told Aunt Sarah, "they should dress all of those men in bib overalls and dash liquor on them. Then put one of those dumb railroad watches in every man's bib pocket and have me run into them one at the time. If the right man grabs me, I think I might know him. But sending me pictures of a bunch of big dirty ugly old railroad men ain't going to help. And, we'll spend the rest of our days right here in this wonderful City of Brotherly Love."

Uncle Frank responded in his typical Uncle Frank fashion, "Jus' hush yo fuss now, boy. 'Stead a' wastin' yo time whinin' and accusin' somebody else for yo troubles, git yosef down on yo knees and ask de good Lawd to show you dis man. Yo see de

168

Lawd knows 'xactly who dis man is. And, de good book done say ask whatevah yo wants and he's gone see dat you gits it. Dat's bout de only way I sees dat you gone know dis man."

Jubal didn't know how to pray. And he sure didn't feel like praying. But that night the boy knelt by the side of his bed the way he had seen it done in pictures and gave praying his best shot.

Chapter 30: The Silhouette

Jubal found the letter address to him. The letter was inside a larger envelope of photos that Sheriff Dunbar addressed to the boy. The boy read,

Dear Jubal,

There are two hundred and seven photographs in this package. Only men who are five foot ten inches or taller were photographed. Skinny men were also excluded. To make your job as easy as possible we have attempted to include only those who logically could be the man who grabbed you. We have records to show that one hundred twenty of the men in these photographs recently purchased watches like the one you took from the man who grabbed you the night of the explosion. Four out of these one hundred and twenty men cannot account for the whereabouts of the watch they purchased. These four men are our prime suspects at this time.

I know that this is a tough job, but it would be great if the man you identify, happens to be one of these four men. So take your time and see if you recognize one of the men. Thank you and good luck.

Your friend,

Sheriff Bob Dunbar

Jubal had a hard time getting started. Everyone else at the house including all the Clarks were equally as interested in the pictures. Everybody picked out their favorite candidate, and several bets were made. It wasn't until Jubal took the entire stack to his room and closed the door that he got a chance to study the photos seriously. But it didn't seem to matter. The more the boy starred at the faces the more impossible the task

171

became. The longer he stared at the men, the more their pictures looked alike and the sicker he became.

When they moved him North, the boy took his night pot along. Miraculously the boy had not needed the pot since he came to Philadelphia. Jubal had not suffered one single headache in northern hemisphere. And, the North, the boy pleasantly discovered is full of bathrooms. Now, however, he slid the pot from beneath his bed and threw up. Aunt Sarah heard the boy heaving and came to check.

"Listen, Jube," she said, "you get yoself in dat bed and don't worry no mo bout no pictures dis night. In de mornin' Aunt Sarah gone fix you a nice breakfast."

Aunt Sarah was true to her word. The next morning the boy awoke to the unmistakable aroma of country ham frying. In addition to the ham, he was served grits, hot homemade biscuits and a cereal bowl filled with red- eyed gravy. "Wow! What a breakfast," the boy said with a flourish, "That was wonderful, Aunt Sarah. Now, I'm going back in there and find the man who grabbed me."

"Dat's zakely what I wants you to do, chile," She replied.

An hour later, Jubal selected number one hundred twenty-nine and laid him aside, just as he had all hundred twenty-eight photos before. Suddenly the boy remembered something. He picked up one hundred twenty-nine again.

"Uncle Frank, Aunt Sarah, Emily, everybody! I've found him! I've found him!" The boy ran through the apartment waving the photo and yelling.

Aunt Sarah grabbed the boy and said, "Praise de Lawd, chile. Is you sho?"

"Yes, yes, look here. Right there, that's him. See here he is. That's the man right there!"

Of course the others didn't have the slightest notion what "right there" or "see here" meant.

"What makes you so sure Jubal?" Emily asked. "Last night you said you couldn't tell one from another." Everyone was throwing the same question at the energized boy now.

"That was before I ate Aunt Sarah's fantastic breakfast," the boy responded only half playfully.

Uncle Frank joined the group wanting to see. But when he barged in front of Aunt Sarah, she shoved him roughly out of her way. It was the first time Jubal had ever seen Aunt Sarah shove anybody, but she was smelling her ticket home now, and she wasn't letting anybody or anything stand in her way. Finally everyone settled down enough to listen while the boy explained.

"It's his ears. You see, look right here, one ear is bigger than the other. I never saw the man's face, but I got a real good hard look at his ears. I remember looking up, straining to see his face. It was real cloudy about that time and all I could see was the outline of the man's head and ears against the night sky. While he was holding me I remember thinking, "Man, one of your ears is bigger than the other. I meant to make a wisecrack about it later, but I had a lot of other things on my mind at the time."

"Yes, yes, Jubal, you're right, " Emily agreed gleefully. "That man's right ear is much bigger than his left."

"Mussa been a prize fighter," Uncle Frank added.

"Yes, yes, that could account for it," Emily agreed.

"This is wonderful, Jubal. That was very clever of you to notice that," Emily complimented the boy.

"Come here, child, and let me hug you," Aunt Sarah insisted.

"Are you absolutely sure, Jubal? Because if you are, we need to get on the phone to the sheriff's office." Emily seemed to be as eager as the others to get back to North Carolina.

"Yes, I'm sure."

"I think we should take just a couple more minutes," Emily now suggested. "Let's take a quick look at all the other photographs, just to make sure there are no other men with mismatched ears."

Each of them, with the exception of Uncle Frank, took a batch of the photos and within minutes, they determined that Jubal's man was the only one with mismatched ears.

Within a minute, Emily had deputy Purvis on the line. She handed Jubal the receiver. The boy heard the familiar voice of Randy Purvis, "Jubal is that you?"

Jubal told him the story of one hundred twenty-nine's ears. Randy responded with the glad news that number one hundred twenty nine was one of their four prime suspects. "If this turns out to be our man you deserve a medal," Randy told the happy boy.

"Never mind the medal, just send the van," the boy responded.

Chapter 31: The Homecoming

The Philadelphia transplants were hoping for word that the police had proven that Albert Caswell was the man who grabbed Jubal on the night of the explosion. But the call on Thursday only told them that Jubal's father and Melinda Brandon would meet them at the railroad station in Centerville on Saturday night. The quartet of homeward bound Fallstonians caught the train in Philadelphia at three p.m on the 20th of December 1941. The train was packed with men in uniform. Jubal didn't object to being with all the military, but he was nervous about what might be happening at home. He didn't look forward to the ordeal of going to court and explaining his part in the case. He was very shaky by the time the train pulled into the station at Centerville.

The Centerville Station turned out to be even more packed with men in military uniform than the 30th Street Station in Philadelphia had been or the train had been. Jubal now understood, perhaps for the first time, how Centerville got its name. Major north-south and east-west rail lines met, merged and diverged at Centerville. While there were no military bases actually located very near Centerville, a large percentage of the servicemen changed trains there in order to reach their bases, several of which were located in North Carolina. During the war, the city of Centerville became famous for its hospitality to stranded, lonely servicemen. It was customary for Centerville citizens to take one or two servicemen home for meals, fellowship and even a place to sleep if needed.

But tonight Centerville was also buzzing with local news. Jubal spotted his father first, then Melinda Brandon. The couple were waving and shoving their way through the crowd to reach them. There were hugs all around before the three women were off to claim the luggage, leaving Jubal's father to break the news to Uncle Frank and the boy that Albert Caswell was dead.

"Albert Caswell? The man who grabbed me? Dead?"

"Yes, son. His body was found yesterday morning. We thought about calling and telling you that before you caught the train, but we figured it was just as well that you didn't hear about it until you got home. At least you guys won't have to testify against him now."

"What happened? How did he die?"

"Someone killed him, son. Hunters found his body. He had been shot several times."

"Why wasn't he in jail?"

"Because the police had no probable cause to arrest him. To date, police have not established that any crime has actually been committed. Caswell was picked up for questioning and asked to explain where he was on the night of the locomotive explosion. Caswell came up with a rather weak alibi, claiming he was on a fishing trip at that time. But he failed to come up with the names of any witnesses who could verify his story. And when asked about the watch he'd recently bought, Caswell told the interrogating officers that he'd thrown the worthless watch in the river on that very same fishing trip."

"Why was he killed? Who would want to kill him?" The boy was becoming more upset by the minute.

"He was probably killed because he knew too much. Someone must have been afraid that if Albert Caswell talked, they, too, could be arrested," the boy's father told him.

The boy knew now that he was past the point of no return. He would have to throw up very soon; he told his father, who swiftly steered him away from the crowd. There were passenger cars on both sides of them, so the boy had to use the space between the cement walkway and the rail cars.

When he was feeling better, Jubal asked, "Why did you bring us home if the killer is still loose?"

"Uncle Frank has never ever seen this other man. And you never got a real good look at him either. With Caswell dead, the other man doesn't have to worry about you or Uncle Frank. You two had a hard enough time identifying Albert Caswell and he was right in your face. And you had Caswell's watch to boot. Now that poor Albert Caswell is not going to do any talking, I don't think the man is going to be worrying about you two."

"So, you're saying, with Mr. Caswell dead, Uncle Frank and I don't have anything to worry about?"

176

"Yes, son, that's the way we see it. You and Uncle Frank were the only people who could identify Caswell. And Caswell was the only person who could identify the other killer or killers. Understand?"

"But I did see the man. He was pretty close to me when I shot at him. And Brodus and Thad saw him, too, didn't they?"

But even if you guys all saw this man, it isn't likely that any of you could make a positive identification, based on what you have told us. Yes, see what I mean? And besides, we don't know where to start looking for this man. This guy might not even be a railroad man. Caswell can't tell on him now, and the killer knows that you don't know who he is. See what I'm saying?"

"You're saying the killer don't care if we live or die, right?"

"Well, I wouldn't put it quite that way, but I think you've got the idea. Come on, men, let's find the ladies. We're taking you heroes out to Cameron's for barbecue," Mason told them.

Mason got Uncle Frank and Aunt Sarah settled in the colored people's dining room, and the boy watched while his father and the ladies ate. Jubal would have to sleep before he could eat again. Mason Scott had to stop his pickup several times on the way home for the boy to heave.

"Sooner or later they're going to catch the other killer or killers," Mason said to Emily as he was driving her home to Fallston. "Caswell's wife is cooperating fully with the police investigation. Molly Caswell admits that her husband was probably there when the locomotive exploded. And she also concedes that her husband could have blown up the locomotive. She believes that her husband knew enough about steam locomotives to blow one up without getting himself blown up. But she steadfastly claims that her husband could not and would not kill the crew of the engine."

After Emily Clark was dropped off at her home in Fallston, and father and son were on their way to the farm, Mason said, "I hope you'll be all right in the morning. Melinda is coming to spend the day with us tomorrow. She'll be here in time for breakfast."

177

Late that night the boy with the sick headache lay in bed thinking about   poor Mr. Caswell and his grieving family. "Because of me," Jubal was thinking, "Mr. Caswell is dead." Then Jubal thought of all the soldiers he had seen that day. How many of them will die and how many of them will kill someone else before the war is over? This thought made his head hurt even more. He had to think of something more pleasant than war and death. Then he began to think of Melinda Brandon. She was coming here in the morning. For breakfast? Wow! Why? Who was she coming to see?

In no time at all the boy's ego took charge. Hadn't he gotten sick and ruined his own homecoming?   And didn't Aunt Sarah always spoil him after he'd been sick? The boy was sure that Melinda and Aunt Sarah talked about that subject this very night while they were picking up their luggage. Now Melinda was about to spoil the boy with a visit first thing in the morning. On that sweet note Jubal Scott fell asleep.

Chapter 32: The Interlude

Melinda Brandon arrived at precisely eight the next morning. This time Jubal was careful to conceal himself behind the curtain of his bedroom window. This time, however, he didn't need to hide. Melinda never looked in the boy's direction. Jubal, however, noticed that she was more beautiful than ever.

Mason Scott suddenly appeared in the yard. The boy watched as the two greeted each other with a hug. Then they walked hand in hand toward the house without so much as a how do you do in Jubal's direction. The message of the scenario was evident: Melinda hadn't come to see him at all. The boy then reverted to another thing in which he excelled. He was an expert pouter. He quickly jumped back into bed and pulled the covers up over his head.

A couple of minutes passed, and he heard Aunt Sarah call, "Breakfast's ready." Mason Scott opened the boy's door, gave the lump in the bed a quick look and closed the door. Through the transom over his door, the boy could smell the bacon, hear the dishes rattling, and worst of all, hear the sound of laughter.

As soon as his father and Melinda left for Sunday school, Jubal went down and drowned his sorrows in pancakes and syrup. He noticed that Aunt Sarah was closing down the kitchen. "Dove and Brodus are coming heah to pick us up for church in a few minutes. Is deah anything else you want fo I go?" she asked.

"Yes ma'am, I want to know what I'm supposed to do for dinner."

"Yo pappy and Miss Melinda gone be back. They'll be taking you over to Miss Callie's again for dinner after church," Aunt Sarah said on her way out.

"Well, I hope it won't be too much of a bother to them," Jubal said to the back of the closed door.

At least Jubal didn't have to worry about Albert Caswell this Sunday morning. Mason Scott had even dismantled Uncle Frank's alarm system at Aunt Sarah's insistence. Now the boy was in the mood for more serious pouting, but there was no one to impress with his misery but himself. It was then that the boy began to realize that for him the worst was finally over. Of course, the down side of this was that he probably no longer needed anyone else's sympathy or protection. The boy wasn't at all sure what that meant in terms of his future, since he was no longer needed to identify the other man. But wait a minute. Wasn't he the only person besides Brodus and Thad who had actually seen this other man? And didn't Brodus and Thad admit that they could not identify the man if they were to see them again?

Jubal was thinking, "I saw the little man. He was only fifteen feet from me when I pulled the bell rope and the trigger of the twelve-gauge shotgun. I talked to him. I heard his voice. He shot at me and I shot at him. We should know each other real well by now. If he's the real killer, like everybody now says, then what am I doing here by myself now. Am I missing something? What's so different now? What makes Papa think that the killer is going to leave me alone?" Jubal was making himself sick all over again.

"Calm down now. Think, boy," he told himself. His train of thought was now like boxcars loaded with empties. But it finally came to him. "Like Papa said, the difference is the watch and the physical contact I had with Albert Caswell. I felt Albert Caswell and smelled him. Then there was the bib overalls he was wearing, and Melinda's knowing that her husband didn't wear bib overalls. Even the railroad police knew that the watch I took did not belong to one of the locomotive crew.

"This other guy? I only saw him once and I was doing several things at that time. I didn't have time to stare. No. He could be any one of a billion small men in the world. Nobody's gonna take pictures and record the voices of every little man in the world. Even Miss Callie ain't got that kind of connections or that much money. If by some wild chance I would hear and recognize the man's voice, so what? This man no longer has a partner in crime to worry about. There is no one to squeal on him. It would be my word against his. No. The killer is smart. If he comes after me again I just might recognize him. And if he's unlucky enough to let me live the second time, it could be the end of him. All the man has to do is stay away from me and he's home free. I'm good at causing people problems. I scared poor Mr. Peterson half to death and got Mr. Caswell killed. Papa's right, I'm not enough of a threat for the killer to risk getting himself killed. I'm just a nobody again."

For the first time in Jubal's life he talked himself out of a sick headache.

School had closed for the Christmas holidays and would not restart until January 5, 1942. Jubal decided to use his new-found freedom by cashing in on his former celebrity status. He considered himself a combat veteran, one who survived the war. Now that he is back home he intends to tell his war stories to anyone who will listen. He visited everyone on the farm and half the people in Fallston. He ate in a different home every day and stayed overnight at the home of several friends during those carefree holidays.

It was during this time that he began to take notice of the changes that had taken place in his area since the war began. There was the proliferation of radios. Owning a radio was no longer looked upon as a luxury, but rather a patriotic duty. The radio fad was especially popular in the part of the country where the boy lived. Fortunately, for that area, the fad started at the time of year when even the poorest farm hand in the area could scrape up a little extra money. And with Christmas approaching, a radio not only made a nice present; giving a radio was the patriotic thing to do. Almost every tenant house, many still without electricity or plumbing, began keeping up with the war news by battery radio.

Radios broadcast far more than war news. Sports, religion, music, drama, ideologies and entertainment on a scale not previously known soon became an everyday part of farm life. Radio became the vanguard of technology that would in a few short years end farm life as he had lived it.

Another oddity Jubal noticed was the favored status now being granted to the wartime tobacco farmer. Oddly enough in those days, tobacco farmers were exempted from a lot of the rationing that was strictly forced upon the average citizens. Hard-to-get items like gasoline and tires were readily available

181

to North Carolina tobacco farmers. During those days the American government treated cigarettes as if they were important to the health and morale of our nation.

The fact that Jubal was no longer the center of the killer's attention did not mean that the case had been solved. However, thanks to the cooperation of Albert Caswell's widow Molly, Miss Callie's investigators had pieced together a comprehensive profile of Albert Caswell. Caswell apparently had both the knowledge and experience to become certified as a pipefitter. And with the shortage of skilled mechanics now affecting the booming railroad industry, he had ample opportunity as well.

Everyone who knew Albert Caswell also knew that the man had two glaring flaws: whiskey and gambling. In combination, these flaws kept Caswell constantly on the brink of financial as well as social disaster. According to his wife, Albert's fortunes had reached an all-time low just prior to the time of the explosion at Fallston. Molly Caswell recalled eviction notices being served. Threats from collection agents were bombarding them daily. Albert Caswell was in danger of losing everything his family owned, as well as his job. Dramatically, however, just prior to the explosion, a miracle apparently happened. Albert Caswell suddenly paid off all his debts. A streak of luck at the crap game, he told his wife. Such a windfall should have made the man very happy. But as Molly Caswell recounted, "Albert's despondency continued right up to the day he was murdered."

Molly Caswell admitted that she should have picked up on the apparent disconnect between her husband's apparent good fortune and his ongoing state of depression. "But to be truthful," she said to Miss Parsons' investigator, "I was so happy to be out of debt, that I simply did not care. For the first time in our married life we had a good car, no debts, and I had money to spend."

"What kind of car did your husband buy?"

"A Buick. Almost new. It's the nicest car we've ever owned."

"What color?"

"Dark green."

Meanwhile, back on the farm, Mason Scott was busying himself with the winter farm activities. Hog killing was strictly a cold-day activity; one that involved everyone on the farm. Except for the hogs, hog killing was a happy time. There were hams, shoulders and bacon to be salted and smoked, chittlins to be cleaned, sausage to be stuffed and plenty of fresh meat to be cooked. Byproducts of hog killing were literally salted away for rainy days. Properly managed, some of this year's hog meat would last until hog killing time next year.

There was repair work to be done on the fences, houses, sheds, wells, water pumps, barns, tools and equipment. Wood had to be cut, gathered, split and hauled to the tobacco barns for next summer's curing. But the most dreaded job of all was clearing land for the infamous tobacco plant bed. It is impossible to overstate the word "clearing." Farmers usually picked the most isolated, roughest, uncultivated, and meanest spot on the farm to clear for the tobacco plant bed.

The forty-foot-square plot of virgin land would not be merely cleared; manicured was more descriptive. Not one semblance of leaf, grass, root, thorn, weed, or thistle was allowed to survive. The task called for raking, grubbing and then grubbing and raking again and again. This is where the concept of clean rooms used in today's laboratories must have originated. Finally, the tiny, near microscopic seeds, sacked and saved from the best of last year's crop were committed to the virgin soil. In April the seedlings would be ready to "set out," and the cycle would continue. Of course, this labor-intensive task is a part of history. Tobacco farmers today buy their seedings ready made directly from the wholesaler's greenhouse.

Mason Scot had great respect for Miss Callie. He was indebted to her for taking care of Jubal and Uncle Frank and Aunt Sarah. He also believed that Callie Parsons was doing the best she could to help Melinda find her husband's killer. But gratitude and respect have their limits. Upon the advice and request of Callie Parsons, Mason had not seen or contacted Melinda for several weeks. And so far as Mason could tell, nothing was happening that would justify such a sacrifice. The man's patience was growing dangerously thin.

Then one cold February night, and not a moment too soon, Callie Parsons called Mason to say that she was on her way over.

Chapter 33: The Motive

Jubal was watching from his window as Edward turned into his yard. He was wearing his heavy coat to keep from freezing in his room. He ran out and escorted his Sunday school teacher into the kitchen. Aunt Sarah's kitchen was the only warm and cozy room in the house when the weather was really cold. Mason Scott was there and greeted Miss Callie. Handshakes were exchanged, and an offer of coffee and cookies was politely refused.

"I came to bring you two up to date on where I'm at with the investigation," Miss Callie began. "First, however, before I get into that, I want to thank you for following my instructions regarding contacts with Melinda. I am sure that staying apart has not been easy for either of you, but I believe that after you hear me out you will agree that it has been the right thing to do.

"I've put a lot of thought plus a considerable amount of research into one particular question in this case." Miss Callie paused for effect. "What is the killer's real motive?   Oh, I know everybody thinks that the killer's motive is tied to the death of Harry Collins, the man in the missing flag case. And everybody may yet be right.   However, I do believe one aspect of that theory: I strongly believe that the killer is counting on that very thing. He wants us to believe that revenge is the motive behind the murder of King, Spencer and Brandon. I now believe that I know the killer's real motive. And I also believe that if I'm right, we may be running out of time.

"When all three crewmen from the missing flag case turned up dead, the motive was obvious. Revenge. A lot of people were probably angry enough to wish them dead. And perhaps there were a few angry enough to kill them. But that's not what actually happened.   Now after thoroughly investigating the revenge motive, I have changed my mind. The facts simply don't back up that theory. I believe that someone paid Albert Caswell a great deal of money, several thousand dollars for his part in the explosion. Caswell's widow agrees. I can't conceive of anyone working at those shops to have that kind of money in the first place. And there were plenty of angry railroad shop men who would help him for free."

Miss Callie had Mason's attention now, but she paused as if to make sure.

Impatient now, Mason prompted, "Then, for heaven's sake, what was the motive?"

"I'm coming to that. But first I want you have the rationale which led me to this conclusion." Callie Parsons was choosing her words slowly and deliberately. "I believe that the killer is well acquainted with Melinda Brandon. Furthermore, I believe that this person is also in some perverted way in love with her. I further believe that the killer will stop at nothing to have her. I believe that the death of Harry Collins and Lacy Brandon's involvement in that tragedy merely presented this crazed individual a window of opportunity to get what he really wanted all along, namely Melinda Brandon. Brandon's involvement in Collins' death was just the break that the clever killer was waiting and hoping for. Now the killer sees a way to eliminate the man in Melinda's life without pointing the finger of suspicion in his direction.

"Lacy Brandon was killed simply because he was the man in Melinda's life. And I don't think the killer will hesitate to kill anyone else that assumes that role in his eyes. In the mind of the killer, Mason, you may be the man in her life right now. That means that you could well become his next victim if you aren't very careful."

Callie Parsons' new theory struck a sour note with Mason Scott, who responded angrily, "I know you mean well, Miss Callie, but I just don't buy this theory of yours. I've never heard Melinda say one word about having any man in her life except her husband. I don't believe there is another man in her life. And that includes me."

"You may be right about that, Mason, but, you're missing my point. I'm not questioning Melinda's chastity or morality in any way. You must admit that Melinda Brandon is a very beautiful, vivacious, attractive and talented woman. You fell for her like a ton of bricks, didn't you?"

186

"Well, er, yes. I wouldn't exactly put it that way, but I suppose you're right, you're right about that."

"Don't you think it's possible that someone else has done the same? I know all this comes as somewhat of a shock, but hear me out, Mason. The other man in love with her may have just the same fate in store for you as he had for poor Lacy Brandon. And that's one of the reasons I came here tonight. I came to warn you. Have there been any attempts on your life recently?"

"I would like to accommodate your theory by believing that I am the man in her life right now. I'm not arguing with you there. But even if that's so, I can't believe that anybody could be crazy or jealous enough to kill any man who looks at Melinda. That just doesn't make any sense," Mason argued.

"Just hold your horses, Mason. I admit that through the eyes of any decent, normal man like yourself, none of this makes sense. But this man is not a normal, decent man. This man is a cold-blooded killer, and we must catch him soon, before he claims his next victim. And in order to catch him, we have to get into the depraved mind of this evil person. Thinking the way he thinks is the only way we are going to be able to stop him. You must know as well as I do that jealousy can be a powerful motive; jealousy can in fact be the most powerful motive of all. Do you remember any time or event lately when you thought someone might have been trying to kill you?"

"No, of course not."

"Now, not so fast, Mason. I know I'm upsetting you, but this is important. Think, man. Have you had a close call while driving, or maybe you thought you heard a shot, you barely escaped having a ton of bricks fall on your head, or anything of that kind?"

"Well, there was one little incident. I was driving home from Martin one night a couple of weeks back and a car ran me off the road right near the bridge over Noble's Creek. The other car suddenly darted out of a side road and was heading right for my truck. To avoid being hit there was nothing for me to do but take to the woods on my left. I knew I was dangerously close to the bridge abutment. Luckily, I knew about the little car path that fishermen use, and I was lucky enough to whip into that path. But that doesn't mean that it wasn't accidental. The driver of that car was probably drunk."

What the driver didn't know probably saved his intended victims life. Mason Scott had a strong knowledge of that spot, because the farm he once owned was located in that area between Martin and Fallston.

"You can call that incident whatever you like, Mason, but I think you were a target. There's a good chance that the man who ran you off the road that night was our killer. Nothing else seems to make sense. The killer is probably laughing his head off right this minute. He has killed four people. And until now, no one has so much as guessed at the real motive behind those killings."

"Do you really expect me to believe that the man who ran me off the road was Lacy Brandon's killer?" Mason shot back angrily. He lost his composure and looked as if he might come down with one of Jubal's headaches. His tone was on the verge of outright disrespect. This was the second time in a conversation with a woman that Jubal had ever witnessed such a thing. On the other occasion Jubal's father was angry with his son and was only taking that anger out on poor Sarah Ruffin.

"What do you think, Jube?" The boy's father had never before asked his son what he thought about anything. By instinct Jubal discovered that blood matters when the fight gets thick. Jubal answered sarcastically, "It sounds to me like maybe we went to Philadelphia for nothing. That's what it sounds like to me."

"Oh, no, no, Jubal," Miss Callie answered, "as long as Albert Caswell was alive, your life and Uncle Frank's were definitely in danger. No, Jubal, believe me, we brought you and Uncle Frank home only when we thought it was safe, and, not one moment before."

The visit was turning ugly. Edward was to pick Callie Parsons up in one hour. Forty of those minutes had passed. And as it turned out, those remaining twenty minutes not only saved the meeting, they also turned the entire case around. If Edward had been parked outside at that moment, Callie Parsons would have walked out of that farmhouse in a huff. Prayer or no

188

prayer, case or no case, Callie Parsons was not accustomed to being shouted at.

Callie Parsons was forced to wait. Mason Scott stood staring into the wall behind Aunt Sarah's stove. There he could see the unpatched holes left by the bullets of a mad man. Somehow that hard evidence was causing the words of Callie Parsons to sink into his own mind. The notion that someone could be insanely in love with Melinda Brandon, jealous enough to kill for her must have suddenly hit home to Mason Scott. He turned to Miss Callie Parsons and said, "Please accept my apology. You're right, a man could easily love her enough to kill if he thought killing would improve his chances of having her."

Miss Callie answered, "I apologize for playing with your emotions, Mason, and yours as well, Jubal, but nothing else seems to make sense. I didn't know any other way to convince you than to be brutally frank. And while I am genuinely concerned that your life 'may' be in jeopardy, I am positive that Melinda is in even graver danger even at this very moment. And that is the main reason I am here tonight. Unfortunately, the only way I know to help Melinda is get Melinda to help us. And we simply must do that before the killer makes his move on her. And that's where you come in.

"I believe that this man, the real killer, is someone well known to Melinda, someone Melinda trusts. And, as you well know, Melinda Brandon is a very trusting woman. She is not going to be easily convinced that one of her trusted friends is a cold-blooded killer. I've already tried. She bluntly refuses to cooperate. But we've got to do something and do it fast."

"What can I do?" Mason wanted to know.

"I believe that you are the one person who can convince Melinda to cooperate. We simply have to pull out all the stops. I'm inviting everyone involved in the case to my house next Sunday afternoon at two o'clock. Feel free to bring Uncle Frank and Jubal along. Sheriff Dunbar, Melinda Brandon and two of my investigators will also be there. I have a plan, but that plan will not work unless we can get Melinda's cooperation."

By the time Mason found his voice, Edward had pulled into the yard.

As they walked Callie Parsons out to her waiting limousine, Mason said, "But you haven't told me what you want me to do."

"Just be there. When the time comes, you'll know what to do."

Chapter 34: The Turning Point

At the outset of the meeting, Miss Parsons gave a general overview of the case. She explained that she now believes that jealousy was the real cause of Lacy Brandon's death. Thankfully, for Mason Scott she did not explain exactly how she had arrived at this conclusion. She then reviewed the profile of Albert Caswell that his widow provided. To this point, the meeting brought no surprises to the Scotts. Mason and Jubal had already heard this very lecture, almost verbatim.

Miss Callie introduced Mr. Charles Amater and Miss Alice Coley of the North State Investigation Agency. Jubal was thinking, "That man was hired in spite of his looks." Mr. Amater was short, fat and bald. His glasses looked as if he wore them to keep his eyes from falling out. Conversely, Jubal could easily see that Alice Coley had obviously been hired because of her looks.

"Mr. Amater will now discuss the work he and his people have done to date," Miss Parsons said.

Jubal had become accustomed to the local version of conducting business. The boy found out later from Uncle Frank that the proper term for Mr. Amater's style of presentation was "citified." He began, "Our specific work has centered around a class roll book loaned to us by Mrs. Brandon. For those of you who might not know, it turns out that Mrs. Brandon has been teaching one class per year since 1937 at Centerville College. Each year since these classes began, the popularity of Mrs. Brandon's music appreciation classes have steadily grown in popularity.

"Last year in fact, her class was moved to the college's main auditorium, and registration for her class was offered to the pubic. More than one hundred non-students audited her class this past semester. Audited her class for a hefty fee, I might add. The names of those not-for-credit students attending Mrs. Brandon's most recent class are now being passed to each of you."

A nod from Amater had the effect of setting that process in motion. Miss Coley immediately stood and began handing out a list of names to each person present. Amater paused and waited for the papers to stop rattling before continuing. "Now that we are all on the same page, are there any questions?" Silence.

"Thank you, Mr. Amater." Callie Parsons was speaking again. "I believe that our killer's name is on the list each of you now have before you." A variety of gasps, gulps and shocked expressions followed. However, for us to have a chance of identifying this person before he strikes again depends heavily upon what Melinda can tell us about several of the people on the list."

All eyes were on Melinda Brandon. Finally, reluctantly she began, her voice only a hoarse whisper. "Four weeks ago Miss Parsons asked me to give her the names of those men on this list who I had more than a casual acquaintance with before the start of last year's class. While I respect Miss Parsons, and appreciate what she is trying to do, I also respect the integrity of others, especially those whom I call personal friends. I simply cannot betray their trust in any way unless there is reason to do so. There are four men on this list who fall into the category of what I care to call personal friends. But I certainly don't know anything about any one of these men that would make me suspicious in any way. Therefore, I don't really see the point of these questions. This whole process is making me feel awful. I do believe that Miss Parsons is trying to help me. But I simply c-a-n not do thi--."

"Look, Melinda," Mason Scott's voice interrupted and carried gruffly and loudly across the table. His voice was neither friendly nor reassuring. "If these people are your real friends, then they certainly have nothing to hide or fear from anyone in this room. If these characters, these friends of yours, are innocent, as you assume, then no real harm is going to be done. Miss Parsons here is merely trying to get at the truth. Why does Miss Callie's need to ask you these hard questions? Let me tell you what I believe. I believe that if you knew even half of what I feel for you, then you'd also know why Miss Callie's theory is worth checking out. I speak from experience. I had feelings for you the moment we met. One of these men, no maybe all of these men, are in love with you, too. But what if one of those men doesn't love you same way that I love you?

"I believe that one of these men killed your husband. I also believe that that same man meant to kill my son. And, thanks to Miss Parsons, I now believe that one of them tried to kill me, too. While it would be almost the greatest thing in the world to know that you loved me, to know that you would be happy with me would be the greatest. Do you think you could be happy with the person who killed your husband?"

Jubal knew from that instant that love can make a fool of a man. Tears were streaming down his father's face now. Jubal hadn't seen anything like that since his mother's funeral. Melinda Brandon's reaction came swiftly.

"Go ahead and investigate all you want to," Melinda shouted, "but, if what Mason says is true, then I'm the one who's guilty of killing my husband. Please get my coat. I really must be going."

Miss Callie followed Melinda to the door. The old lady must have heard a chair squeak. When she looked back she noticed that Mason Scott had risen from his seat. She immediately motioned for him to sit. The door closed softly after the two women. The library was now a tomb. Finally the sheriff got up and crossed over and sat down in Miss Callie's empty chair beside his friend. The boy now also understood why his father usually had so little to say. Whenever he did speak, he almost always wound up in trouble.

Miss Callie opened the door and everyone in the room became silent. All eyes were on Miss Callie now. The sheriff, remembering that he was now seated in the hostess' chair, started lumbering to his feet. Miss Callie motioned for him to stay put. Instead she took the seat that Melinda Brandon had vacated.

"She'll be all right," Miss Callie said. "She's such a lady. She just hates the idea that one of her close friends could be capable of doing something like this. But as I explained to her outside, our Lord had a similar problem. I told her to remember who betrayed him. She has gone to the bathroom to fix her face.

She'll be back in a few minutes. Meanwhile, why don't we all take a break for refreshments."

Melinda returned. It was almost as if a new meeting was about to begin. The atmosphere had changed drastically. A new lighthearted aura settled over the room and the people in it. Jubal was remembering the coolness after a storm while he and Uncle Frank were curing tobacco. Once Callie Parsons seated herself at the table again, everyone else quickly followed suit and the meeting continued.

"Melinda, my dear, I see that you have four names checked here on your list."

"Yes, ma'am, four names. Those four men are all friends of mine and they all audited my last music appreciation class."

"Well, what I would like to do now with your permission, of course, is to simply ask you a few questions about each of these four. And I would remind you that Miss Coley here will be taking notes on these questions and your answers. Is that understood?"

Melinda Brandon answered with a slight nod.

"Let me assure you further, that each of the people in this room will treat anything that you say as confidential. Are you ready, my dear?"

Melinda gave another almost imperceptible nod and the questioning began.

"Let's take these four in alphabetical order. My very first question will apply to each of them. Jubal and the others have described the man we are looking for as a small man. Consequently we are only interested here with men who are small, say the size of Mason Scott. Is that right, Jubal?"

"Yes ma'am, the man who shot at me was about the size of my father."

Now, Melinda, what can you tell about Mr. Thomas Evans?"

Chapter 35: Thomas Evans, the Grocer

Melinda Brandon began, "Tom Evans owns the grocery store in my neighborhood. My husband and I have been buying our groceries from Tom for more than ten years. And I'm still buying my groceries from Tom's store. My husband and I have been good friends with Tom Evans for more than ten years. We knew him for years before he opened his own store. Tom Evans is a very nice man. That's about all I can tell you about him."

"Why do you think he audited your class?"

"Tom likes classical music. I guess that's why."

"How do you know that he likes classical music?"

"Everyone who visits his store can answer that. Tom keeps the radio in the back of his store playing all the time. And that radio is always tuned to the classical music station in Richmond."

"Did Tom Evans tell you ahead of time that he was going to audit your class?"

"No. I was surprised to see his name on the list the registrar gave me. It was a large class, and I thought that there might be two Tom Evanses. But when I looked at the class that first night, there he was."

"So you had no idea that he was planning to take your class?"

"No, I honestly didn't. But now that you're asking me about it, I do remember that the two of us talked about the class on several occasions. But he never actually mentioned that he was planning to enroll."

"How did he behave in class? Did he ask questions, interrupt, or enter into class discussion often, that sort of thing?"

"No, I don't recall him saying anything or asking questions during class, but when I'd go to the store, he and I did get into some pretty lively conversations about the class material. He was very knowledgeable and keenly interested in music."

"Have you seen Mr. Evans often since your husband's death?"

"Yes, about as often as usual, two or three times a week I suppose."

"Have you noticed any change in the way he talks or acts towards you since your husband's death?"

"Absolutely not. Of course, like countless other friends of ours, Tom has been very supportive."

"Supportive. Supportive in what way?"

"Things like flowers, cards, phone calls, that sort of thing."

"How about candy, offers to take you out to lunch, stuff like that?"

"No. Nothing like that."

"Take your time now, Melinda. I know you don't like this. But it's very important that we know what you know, even if you think that what you know is none of our business. I want to remind you again. If Tom Evans or any of these men are just as you say and obviously believe, simply a good friend, then no harm is going to be done to that friendship."

"There is one thing," Melinda said. "Tom called me up one night about two months ago and asked me if I would like to go with him to a concert in Raleigh. He explained, as I already knew, that the North Carolina Symphony would be featuring several outstanding guest artists."

"I told Tom that I was flattered by his offer, but I explained that I didn't feel like getting involved with social activities at this time."

"What was his reaction?"

"He told me that he understood, but added that if I needed a friend or anything at all, to give him a call, or words to that effect."

"And he hasn't attempted to make another date with you or anything of that sort since that one call?"

"No," Melinda answered sharply. "I know all of you are trying to help, but I've already told you that I don't suspect any of these men. I am proud to have each of these four men as friends. I've already told you that I have never had reason to suspect the motives of any one of them. Isn't that good enough?"

"For your sake, I hope you are right, my dear. If that turns out to be the case, I'll be the first to say that I'm sorry for putting

196

you through this," Miss Callie answered firmly. "I have only one more question about Tom Evans. In your opinion, is Mr. Evans a wealthy man?"

"I honestly do not know. I do know that Tom has been divorced for several years. I imagine a lot of his money went for child support and alimony."

"How do you know this?"

"Mostly from Lacy. Tom and Lacy were pretty close. According to Lacy a great many took advantage of Tom's goodness. You run a store yourself, Miss Parsons, so you know how that works better than I. For those reasons I don't believe that Tom Evans has a lot of free capital hanging around."

"You're doing just great, Melinda. I think that we can move on to Dr. Lester Glassman now."

"Well, I'm happy and relieved to say that Dr. Glassman will not be dragged through all this. He is as big as Sheriff Dunbar." Everyone in the room except the sheriff laughed.

"All right, let's move onto Wally Meecham. What can you tell us about him."

"Before we talk about Wally, there is one more thing I think you should know about Tom Evans. Many, or perhaps, most of Tom's regular customers worked at the Centerville Railroad Shops. And when Lacy got involved with the death of Mr. Collins, Tom lost a lot of customers. Lacy went to Tom and offered to take our trade someplace else. Tom became very upset with Lacy. He told Lacy that we were his best customers. Tom said that most of the customers who stopped trading with him were deadbeats and owed him large sums of money. 'Good riddance,' I believe were Tom's words. Tom told Lacy to let him know when we had a better excuse for trading elsewhere. As far as I know that's the last Lacy or I ever said or thought about changing grocers."

"I see why you have been so reluctant to talk about your friends. Mr. Evans certainly sounds like a man who can be trusted," Miss Parsons said. "Please keep in mind that we are looking for a very cunning, clever and ruthless killer. We simply have to find him before he decides to strike again. Let's go on with Mr. Meecham.

Chapter 36: Wally Meecham, the Mailman

Wally Meecham has been our mailman for about three years. Dear Mr. Meecham. He always has a smile and a good word for everyone in the neighborhood. Everybody likes Mr. Meecham. I really don't know what else I can say about him. "

"Why do you think Mr. Meecham took your class? Is he a classic music lover, too?"

"No, I don't think so. But, Mr. Meecham seems to have a natural curiosity about almost everything."

"Did he just show up in your class unexpectedly like the others, or did you know in advance that he was going to enroll?"

"He often kidded me that he would show up in my class one day, but I was still surprised when he actually did."

"I take it then you and Meecham have talked a lot. Is that right?"

"No, not really. There was a time right after his wife died, that he seemed to be down. During that time, all of us in the neighborhood did what we could to cheer him up."

"When was this?"

"Wally's wife was killed not very long after Harry Collins was killed. Maybe a couple of months, something like that. It had to be sometime during the fall of 1940."

"Did you say killed? How was Mrs. Meecham killed? Do you know?"

"Well, yes. Mrs. Meecham was killed when the car she and Wally were riding in ran off the road and crashed into the woods. Wally was thrown clear of the wreckage, but his wife died in the crash. According to Wally, an oncoming car veered across the center of road and he lost control of his car while attempting to avoid a head-on collision."

"Yes, I see how Mr. Meecham would have been distraught after an experience like that," Miss Callie remarked.

"You say you and the neighbors did what you could to try and cheer him up. What specifically did you do to help Mr. Meecham?"

"Nothing really much stands out in my mind now. But I do remember attending his wife's funeral. And I remember that I baked Wally a cake for his birthday and took it by his house. I'm sure I sent him a sympathy card. That's about it."

"You say you baked a cake and took it to Meecham's house?"

"Yes. I remember it was raining when I got to his house and I had a heck of a time, what with the wind and the rain and the cake all at once. Wally came out to my car with an umbrella. And at his insistence I went into his house long enough as I remember him saying, to put myself back together. I wound up staying for more than an hour. His wife had been dead for no more than a month and I knew that he must have been very lonely. I stayed for coffee and a piece of my own cake. We had a nice talk."

"What did you talk about?"

"Oh, about his paintings, mostly. He had quite a collection of oil paintings, many of which to my surprise, Mr. Meecham had painted himself."

"Did you know before that night that Mr. Meecham was an artist?"

"No. I had no idea. I knew that he could talk on most any subject. But, no, I didn't have any idea that he actually had artistic ability, too."

"He gave you one of his paintings that night, didn't he?"

"Yes, he did. I kept insisting that I had to go. He insisted that I take my pick from the more than thirty or forty paintings he showed me. How did you know that he gave me a painting?"

"The landscape in your den has his signature on it." Miss Callie answered casually.

"I insisted on paying Mr. Meecham for the painting, but he wouldn't hear of it. I know that you're about to ask, but my relationship with Mr. Meecham hasn't changed since Lacy has been gone. Actually, I have seen less of Mr. Meecham since my husband died than I did before. I seem to be constantly on the go. No. Mr. Meecham was nice to me then and he's nice to me now. That's all. No phone calls, no offers to date or anything like that."

"Then you're sure you have nothing more you can tell us about Mr. Meecham?"

"What about Mr. Meecham's financial status? Does he live in an expensive home?"

"No. Wally's home is very nice, but not a mansion like this by any means. I would say that his house is average for Centerville. But now that you mention finances, I do remember hearing a rumor that Wally had taken out a rather large insurance policy on his wife within the last year of her life. Rumor had it that the insurance company did more investigating than the police did. But in the end I heard that the insurance paid double because of the accidental coverage."

"Very good, Melinda, this information may prove to be very helpful. Is there anything else about Mr. Meecham?"

"No. I feel like I may have said too much already."

"By the way, did Mr. Meecham know that you were bringing him a cake before you actually arrived at his house?"

"Why, yes, I do remember calling Wally and telling him that I was on my way over. I wanted to make sure that he was at home before I loaded a chocolate cake in the rain."

"What time was this? Do you remember?"

"Yes, it was about five in the afternoon."

"What was his response when you told him you were bringing him a cake?"

"He said I should wait until it stopped raining. He said he didn't want his cake ruined."

"What time did it stop raining?"

"I'm not sure. But I do remember that it was still raining when I left his house. I remember Wally saying that I should wait until it stopped raining.

"Wait at his house you mean?"

"Well, yes. He argued that it was one thing if his chocolate cake got wet, but it would be a real shame if my my painting was ruined."

"How did you solve the problem?"

"I left the painting at his house and went home. I didn't feel right being at his house after dark, and it was getting late."

"When and how did you finally get the painting?"

"Wally knocked on my door that night around nine o'clock. The rain had stopped. The door bell rang. Remember, we were getting a lot of cranks calls and all sorts of things left on our porch along then. Lacy was away at the time, and I called to ask who it was before opening the door. Wally called saying something to the effect that he was the art delivery man. I opened the door and he handed me the painting."

"Did he ask to come in?"

"No. I thanked him and he left."

"You were home alone at the time, is that correct?"

"Oh, no. Several of the people from our church choir were at my house. We were practicing for a special that following Sunday."

"And Wally Meecham has not been inside your house since then?"

"That's correct."

"And you haven't been inside his house either?"

"That's also correct."

"Then, we can go on to this last name on our list. What can you tell us about John W. Russell?"

Chapter 37: John Russell, the Mechanic

"John Russell owns and operates the garage and gas station where we, that is I er--- I buy my gas and have my car serviced. My husband and I have been trading with John for quite a number of years. Actually, of the four men John Russell was the only one I considered to be a close personal friend of my husband. Lacy and John had similar tastes in many areas, sports, movies and especially music. Both loved country-western. They often went fishing and hunting together and the two of them took in all of the country-western shows that barnstormed through our area. He even got Lacy to take up golf shortly before he was murdered. No, I simply can't imagine John being involved in my husband's death," she said with finality. And, no he hasn't made any advances toward me either before or since my husband's death."

"Do you know if John Russell lost business because of the flag incident? I would assume that Russell faced a problem similar to that experienced by Evans at the grocery," Miss Callie said.

"I suppose he did in a way. But John was apparently in a much better position to absorb such losses as opposed to Tom Evans," Melinda answered.

"Why do you say that?"

"Well, for one thing, John owns his own shop. Tom Evans rents the building he uses for his store."

"Yes, I can see how that might make a difference," Miss Callie agreed. But you used the phrase, 'in a way.' Is there another reason?

"I honestly don't know. That's what makes this so difficult. I'm saying things about my friends that may or not be true. I will say the John 'seems' financially better off than Tom Evans. Poor Tom works all the time. John works when John wants. John finds time for every fishing, hunting, sporting and every musical event that happens along. John charges me a mere fraction of what I would pay anyone else to do the work he does for me.

There are times when he absolutely refuses to accept any pay at all," Melinda concluded.

Miss Parsons recognized that Melinda was becoming upset again. "Your reluctance to talk about your friends has become clearer as we've heard you answer my questions. It is obvious that you think highly of each of them. I continue to believe, however, that benefits from the statements you've providing far outweigh any damage you may have done. From what you've said so far about John Russell, I'm most puzzled as to his motive for auditing your class. You say that your husband and John both preferred country music to classic. Is that right?"

"Yes, that's true."

"John Russell, was one of your husband's closest friends. But you and John shared very little in common. Is that correct?"

"Yes, that's true."

"In that case, why do you think John Russell signed up for your class?

"John always dreamed of becoming a songwriter. Country song writer to be more specific. But he didn't know the first thing about music. John is, if I do say so, somewhat strange. John got it through his head that since I was a music teacher, he could go to my class and learn everything he needed to know about songwriting. Once John Russell makes up his mind about anything, there is no changing it. Furthermore, he'll never admit that my class didn't teach him how to read or write music. But I'm sure that it didn't.

"As I've already said, John believed that my class would turn him into a songwriter. I tried to tell him that my class was not designed for that purpose. Lacy tried to tell him, too. But ole stubborn John had to find that out for himself. John's dream would have been better served in a class structured to teach songwriting. But he stuck it out and still claims that my class helped him a lot. That's about all I can tell you about John Russell except that he is somewhat of a flirt. It's just his way. He never married, and to tell the truth, I don't think John ever had a steady girlfriend. He just likes to flirt.

"Has John Russell asked you to go out with him? You say he's quite a flirt."

"Well yes, he has asked me, but I haven't taken him seriously. I'm sure John was only kidding the couple of times he did ask me to go out with him."

"Tell me about one of the times when John asked you out."

"I took my car to John's shop to be serviced about three months ago. I was planning to walk home and leave my car. It was only about four blocks to my house. But John wouldn't hear of it. He insisted that he give me a ride. On the way to my house he said that I ought to be getting out more, and in particular needed to be going out with him. When I asked him why did he think I needed to go out with him, he said because you don't need to be going out with anybody else."

"And that's it? That's all he said?"

"No. He said he was picking me up at eight o'clock sharp the next morning, which is what he did."

"And where did you two go at eight o'clock the next morning?"

"To his shop where I picked up my car and went to work."

"And that was it?"

"That was it."

This time everyone laughed and the meeting was over.

After supper that night Mason walked Melinda to her car. Jubal, of course, was watching them closely. He could easily see that they were holding hands. And from the way they embraced he could almost swear that they were kissing, too. The boy clapped his hands and said, "Hot dog." He knew that if Mason couldn't have her, neither could he.

Chapter 38: The Reluctant Spy

Jubal was told only that he was to spend the following Saturday with Miss Coley. The boy was so excited at that prospect that he didn't bother to ask questions. He had written in his journal that she was a charmer. Little did the boy realize that he was in for the charm job of his life.

A day with the world's most beautiful detective sounded like pure pleasure to the boy. It began well enough. Miss Coley picked up the unsuspecting boy exactly at eight a.m., and for the next thirty minutes while she drove, they chatted and enjoyed each other's company. As Jubal commented that they were nearing Centerville, the sugar began to wear off their candy-coated conversation. The detective's speech took on the flavor of business.

She told him that the two of them were on a spy mission and that he, Jubal Early Scott, was to play the role of chief spy. His job was to take a look at each of the three suspects on Melinda Brandon's list. As they approached the city limits of Centerville Alice Coley said, "Miss Parsons believes that there is a good chance that one of these three men came to your house and shot at you that Sunday morning. We want you to take a look at each of them and see if you recognize any of them."

"Oh, no, you're not. I've seen enough of that guy to last this kid a lifetime. You might as well take me home right now. What do you people think the killer's gonna do if and when he sees me again. That man came pretty close to killing me the last time we met. I'm not kidding, just take me home."

"Now, calm down, Jubal. I said you were going to get a look at those men, but I didn't say that any of them was going to get a look at you. Now, did I?"

"And just how are you gonna arrange a miracle like that?"

"It's simple really. Everything has been arranged. You will be in no danger whatsoever. My job is to see to that. You trust me, don't you?"

"Oh, I trust you all right. It's the killer that I don't trust."

"Hold your horses just a minute, Jubal, and let me explain. The first thing we're going to do is pay Mrs. Brandon a visit. Let's see. It's almost nine now. She will be expecting us in a couple of minutes. Mr. Meecham, one of the three men we want you to see will be delivering Mrs. Brandon's mail around ten o'clock, give or take ten or fifteen minutes. By that time my car will be parked in Miss Brandon's garage with the door closed so that Mr. Meecham can't see it. We'll be inside with Mrs. Brandon. You simply look out the window and watch Mr. Meecham as he delivers mail to Miss Brandon's box on her front porch. He'll never know you're there. Now, you're not afraid to do that, are you?"

"You say there's no chance that he's gonna see me?"

"That's right. He won't be able to see you. This is what's going to happen. Mr. Meecham puts mail in Mrs. Brandon's mailbox and leaves. After he's gone you tell us if you think you've ever seen him before. It's just that simple."

"And then we can go home?"

"Well, yes and no. We do want you to get a look at the other two men later on if we get the chance."

"I'll do this one. That's all I'm promising. Not right now I ain't."

"I'm not," she corrected.

By the time they turned into Melinda's driveway a few minutes later, Jubal had some of his old bravado back. "We are gonna get these guys this time, ain't we, Miss Coley?"

"Aren't we," Alice corrected. "Yes, we're going to get them, but we don't want you to make any mistake either. As you know, Mrs. Brandon thinks that this is a waste. She does not believe that any of these men are in any way involved in her husband's death. We want you to take your time and make sure before you say anything. The last thing Miss Callie wants is to upset Mrs. Brandon all over again. You were there at that meeting we had a while back. You remember what a hard time Miss Parsons had getting Mrs. Brandon to cooperate, don't you?"

"Yes ma'am, I remember that all right."

"Miss Parsons had an even more difficult time convincing her to go along with our plan for today. We don't want to do anything to mess that up. You do understand, don't you?"

"Yes, ma'am."

"And you can stop calling me ma'am. Alice will do just fine."

Melinda's double-garage doors were open as expected. Melinda's car was occupying one of the two parking spots. Alice pointed out the mailbox, and she drove directly into the garage, where Melinda was waiting. Everything was going just the way Alice Coley explained. Melinda pulled the overhead garage door down. They waited in the car until the door was completely closed before "Good mornings" were exchanged. The usual hugs were omitted. The atmosphere was very business-like. Miss Coley was not a Baptist.

"If you need to go to the bathroom, Jubal, now would be a good time," Melinda suggested bluntly as they passed the small halfbath off the hallway. "Once you're in place, I expect you to stay put until Mr. Meecham comes and leaves."

Jubal indicated that he was taking advantage of the offer by making a left turn into the bathroom. As he entered the bathroom, Melinda added, "Miss Coley and I will wait for you in the den."

When Jubal joined the two women a couple of minutes later, they were talking about the Meecham painting. Jubal was expecting, and hoping that the painting would be as pathetic as one he might paint himself. But much to his disappointment, the painting turned out to be beautiful.

"Here, Jubal," Alice directed, "I want you to sit here. Mrs. Brandon is going to walk out to the sidewalk and then back here to the mailbox on the porch. We can watch her and she'll let us know if we can be seen from the outside looking in."

For her part, Melinda Brandon was saying nothing. Jubal knew that she was either angry or just plain pouting. He was good at recognizing both.

The cheese-cloth curtains kept Jubal from getting a clear view, but he could easily recognize Melinda's pleasant features. The weather was bright, windy and crisp. It was virtually a cloudless morning, and Melinda's front yard was flooded with sunlight. As Melinda walked, Alice asked questions. "Can you see her plainly? Would it be better if you moved over this way a bit? Here, try these binoculars. Do they help?"

Melinda picked up the morning paper which was lying close to the fence marking the boundary between her yard and the one next door. Apparently a delivery boy had thrown the morning paper there sometime earlier. She picked up the paper and went through the motions of reading the headlines. After a minute or so she began to walk back toward her front door. She paused at the mailbox and went through the pretext of checking to see if there was any mail inside. Jubal could hear the box open and close very clearly. Moments later she was back in the den where Alice and the boy anxiously awaited the verdict.

"I'm positive that Jubal can't be seen. While we wait, would either of you care to see the paper?" Melinda offered.

Time passed ever so slowly. No words were spoken for a long, long time in the tension-filled room. Melinda Brandon finally broke the silence.

"This is all so utterly useless and foolish. I don't know why I let myself be talked into anything so stupid as to spy on my friends this way."

By the tone of her voice, Melinda probably had more to say, but Alice cut her off with the news, "Here he comes!"

The boy's heart was about to pound out of my chest. "Is that him?" Jubal managed to whisper.

"Yes, that's our dangerous suspect. That's the infamous Mr. Meecham," Melinda Brandon answered softly, but sarcastically.

As the boy watched the mailman's horizontal approach along and beyond the picket fence, he was thinking to himself, "that little man wouldn't hurt a flea." Meecham opened the gate latch and stepped onto the walkway leading to Melinda's house. However, instead of approaching the house directly, he swung back around and carefully closed the gate behind himself. His movements now were very deliberate, almost like slow motion. He looked up, down and across the street. Mr. Meecham's behavior was sending chills down the boy's spine and Alice Coley into action.

"Does he normally close the gate when he delivers the mail?"

"No. I've never seen him close that gate before." Melinda's voice now contained a slight note of concern. "What do I do if he knocks? If he wants to come in? What a mess!"

"If he knocks answer the door, but don't let him in. Make up something. Tell him you're late for an appointment."

The boy watched Mr. Meecham as he approached directly along his line of sight. The boy's mind went back to that Sunday when he was nearly killed by a gunman as he peered out his kitchen window at home. He was reliving that event and watching the mailman at the same time. As he watched, Wally Meecham, Melinda's harmless mailman, became the shorter of the two men. Harmless Mr. Mailman was looking more and more like the man who shot out the boy's kitchen window."

When the mailman reached in his mailbag the boy knew. Jubal knew beyond any doubt that Mr. Meecham was about to pull out a gun and shoot him dead. The boy began yelling and screaming.

"Help, help, shoot him, kill him, he's going to ki--"

Without taking time off the clock, Alice Coley closed the distance between herself and the boy. She clamped his mouth tight with a ladylike hand, but not in a very ladylike way. Jubal had never kicked a woman before, but, he was kicking one now. The door bell rang. Melinda started toward the front door. Alice pulled a small business-like pistol from her handbag with her free hand. The boy wondered if she was about to shoot him. He immediately stopped kicking and struggling. Somehow, he managed to communicate to Alice that he had gotten control of himself. She let him go as Melinda opened the door.

"Are you all right? I thought I heard somebody yelling bloody murder inside." Jubal had heard that voice before.

"Oh, that was just the radio," Melinda answered causally. "It's happened several times lately. Sometime when I switch the thing on, the volume control goes wacky. That radio must think I'm stone deaf. But thank you for offering to rescue me."

"Since I can't do anything for you, maybe you can do something for me. I've got the worst toothache of my life. Can I

211

use your phone to call Dr. Glassman? I hope he can see me as soon as I finish my route."

There were two telephones in the house. One sat on the night table next to Melinda's bed, and the other was mounted on the wall not six feet from where the boy and his beautiful detective were now standing. Giving the boy the hush signal with one hand, Alice Coley was motioning for Jubal to follow her with the other. By the time Melinda and the mailman entered the room, Alice and the boy were out of sight behind the piano.

"I have Dr. Glassman's number right here in the pad next to the phone," Melinda offered.

"I need his home number. Dr. Glassman doesn't open his office on Saturdays."

"I have that here, too, it's, er-let's see it's 856-W."

The sound the phone made when it came off the hook was deafening amid the otherwise tomblike silence in the acoustically correct room. Meecham answered the operator's "Number please?" with the numerals "856-W." The boy could hear 856-W ringing somewhere. It rang and rang. After ten unanswered rings, Melinda's phone was cradled and the mailman shrugged.

"What are you going to do?" Melinda asked.

"I have to finish my route. I'll try Dr. Glassman again after that. If I can't get him, I'll just have to find someone else to help me," Wally Meecham replied. "In the meantime if you could please get me an aspirin or two. I can bite down on one of those and maybe it will relieve the pain."

"Sure. I'll get you some. Just wait right here. I'll be right back."

"While you're gone," Meecham said, "I'll fish out your mail and leave it here on the table."

The telephone was between the spies hiding place and the table. Jubal reasoned that while Meecham was putting the mail on the table, his back would be turned in his direction. He peeked around the edge of the piano. Luckily there was a houseplant of some kind on a stand nearby, and its foliage offered the boy additional cover. As Jubal watched, Meecham quickly dropped a packet of letters on the table. He then reached further into his mailbag and removed another letter which he slid under the others, making sure that it was on the bottom of the stack. Jubal could hear Melinda's footsteps as she returned with the requested medication.

Melinda handed her mailman a tin box of aspirin. "There must be six or more in this box. Take them along; you may need them. I've got more in the medicine cabinet."

"Thanks, I'm sorry to be such a bother." Meecham placed an aspirin on one of his back teeth and gently closed his mouth. After a slight adjustment, he managed to mumble and nod his approval. Melinda gave him a similar reply, and followed him to the front door, opening it for him. Moments later she was back in the den.

"He's gone," Melinda stormed. "What in the world's gotten into you, Jubal? Do you still think that poor Mr. Meecham was really trying to kill you? He wasn't trying to kill you. The poor man himself was dying with a blasted toothache."

"I hope he fell for that bit about the broken radio dial. That was pretty fast thinking, " Alice Coley congratulated.

"Oh, it was easy. I think if I work with you people much more, I'll soon become a very convincing liar." Melinda was very angry and becoming even more so by the minute. None of the three were operating on the same frequency now.

"Look at your mail. Meecham did something very funny. He deliberately put a piece of mail under the bottom of your letters," Alice said, pointing to the pile of letters.

"Yeah, I saw him do that, too," the boy added. At least Alice and the boy were thinking together again.

"What on earth are you two talking about now? Can't a person at least look at her own mail in private?"

"Just look at your mail, please," Alice insisted.

Melinda angrily snatched up the stack . It contained several letters and cards. She studied the face of each envelope briefly and flipped each aside without comment. When she finally looked at the bottom letter she inhaled loudly enough to indicate shock. "Why, this letter is addressed to Wally T. Meecham," Melinda said. "Wally left this one by mistake."

Alice Coley, Melinda and the boy began talking at once. The room was filled with confusion. In the end both Alice and the boy told the same story: Wally Meecham deliberately placed that envelope, the one addressed to himself, at the bottom of Melinda's stack of mail.

Melinda responded predictably. "Why in the world would Wally do a thing like that I wonder?"

"That is exactly what I have been hired to find out," Alice answered.

Chapter 39: Too Much Mail

For a while, Meecham's mystery letter was the focus of attention, but not nearly long enough to suit the boy. Both women turned on Jubal with a barrage of questions. Eventually, Alice Coley gave way to Melinda, who taking a page out of Miss Callie's book, began to cross-examine the boy.

Melinda was so angry and upset with Jubal that she'd forgotten his name. "What were you yelling and screaming about, boy?"

"Because that man, that Mr. Meecham of yours is the man who tried to kill me once before, that's why! I know he's the man! I'll never forget the way the way the man walked, and when your Mr. Meecham reached in that mailbag the same way he reached for that pistol at my house, I knew it was him!" Jubal was upset too.

"Oh, come on, Jubal, we went through all this before with Rodney Peterson, remember?"

"I remember all right but this Meecham is different. I never got a look at the man I misstook for Mr. Peterson. But I got a real good look at your Mr. Meecham a while ago. Anyway, ain't I the boy who identified Mr. Caswell by one ear, for God's sake?" Jubal's English and moral upbringing were both failing him now. But the point of what he was saying was beginning to have a telling effect on both of the women.

"I'm sorry, Jubal, but I simply can't believe this is happening. I don't know if this is a dream or what," Melinda protested. "Jubal, honey, do you honestly believe that Wally Meecham is the man who shot at you?"

"Yes, ma'am. Cross my heart and hope to die I do. He's the man all right."

"What are we going to do? This is crazy," Melinda moaned.

"Did you know that Dr. Glassman's office was closed on Saturdays?" Alice asked.

"No. Er..., I didn't." The sudden change of subject had a calming effect on Melinda. It gave her something else to occupy her mind. "I never thought about it. But, now that you mention it, I believe that he does have office hours on Saturday."

"Well, we can settle that easy enough," Alice Coley directed. "Give me Dr. Glassman's office number."

"Why do you want his office number. His office is closed on Saturdays, didn't you hear Wally say th--?" Melinda, still somewhat confused, caught the significance of Alice's request and quickly produced the number.

Dr. Glassman's receptionist answered on the first ring. "I'm looking for information really. I'm new in town. I have three children who need to have checkups pretty soon, and I wanted to know if your office is open on Saturdays."

Alice waited patiently while the receptionist apparently went through the office schedule plus a goodly serving of salesmanship. Obviously pressed for name, address and phone number, Alice invented a story. She was new in town and promised to call back once she got settled. Alice hung up the phone and faced an astonished Melinda.

"What do you make of that?" Alice finally prompted.

"Maybe Wally thought that Dr. Glassman's office was closed on Saturdays, because most dentists in town don't have Saturday office hours," Melinda argued weakly.

"Maybe a lot of things. There are enough maybes around here now to make my head swim. But one thing is certain. We've got a potentially explosive and dangerous situation on our hands. Your Mr. Meecham may be as innocent as you want to believe and he wants us to believe, but what if he isn't? We've simply got to take that into account, too."

"What do you suggest? What should I do about the letter?"

"Thankfully, we have a little time. If he is up to something, Meecham is obviously not planning to make a move for the next several hours. I'm betting that later this afternoon he'll be at home and hoping for a phone call from you about his letter. And if you don't call him, he'll probably call you. Of course, we can frustrate whatever he's planning to do if we act fast. You can drive over to his house right now and put his letter in his mailbox. Jubal and I can follow in my car in case anything goes wrong. Write him a note and pin it to his front door. Write

216

something like, I found your letter and decided to deliver your mail for a change. Or something like that. That way we could drive out of town and let Miss Parsons and the police know what's gone on so far."

Melinda Brandon was visibly shaken by all of the clandestine maneuvering. Nevertheless, she began to follow Alice's suggestion. She produced a pad of paper from the desk in the den and made several false starts at composing the note. The wastebasket began to overflow. Finally Alice suggested that she write the note herself on Melinda's typewriter. That way Melinda need only sign the note. This idea prevailed, and the note was typed and snatched out of the machine before Jubal could have gotten the paper in. Melinda left the room to pack for an overnight trip, leaving Alice and the boy alone.

"I don't mean to tell you what to do; Lord knows I am personally in favor of getting away from here right this minute, but don't you think you'd better call Miss Callie or the sheriff or somebody before you let this fish off your hook?" Jubal was using one of Uncle Frank's cliches.

"You are absolutely right, Jube." The boy's beautiful chaperone's face glowed with genuine admiration, and she paused long enough to give the boy a hug and tell him that she loved him before lifting a small black book from her purse. Moments later she was asking someone on the other end of the line if she could please speak with Miss Parsons. The boy listened as Alice Coley gave her client a complete recap of the events of the past hour, including the idea of returning the letter to Meecham's mailbox.

Melinda re-entered the room while Alice Coley was still on the phone. "It's Miss Parsons," Alice said. "She wants to speak with you."

"This is Melinda," she answered weakly and wearily.

Melinda Brandon listened in silence for long periods, punctuated with an an occasional, "Yes I see," or "Yes, I understand," before wordlessly passing the phone to the boy.

"Miss Callie, this is Jubal. Is that you?"

"Yes, this is Miss Callie. Are you all right, son?"

"Yes, ma'am, "I'm fine."

217

"Miss Coley tells me that you are positive that Mr. Meecham is the man who shot at you."

"Yes, ma'am, I'm positive."

"I believe you. Please put Miss Coley on the phone."

After the phone was replaced on its hook, Alice told the others that there had been a change of plans. Alice explained, "Miss Parsons wants us to stay right here in the house and wait. Miss Parsons and I agree that we are in no immediate danger and it would be foolish for us to waste an opportunity to find out what Meecham is really up to. Miss Parsons is to call us back within the hour. If we don't hear from her by that time, we are to get on with our original plan: Deliver the letter and then drive to Fallston.

The boy was all in favor of the Fallston phase of the plan and hated himself for suggesting that they call Miss Callie. There was a clock on the wall above the telephone. The boy began concentrating on the second and minute hands. He took the responsibility of making sure they didn't wait one second past one hour before heading for home sweet home. Meanwhile, Melinda was pacing and Alice was holding Mr. Meecham's letter up to the light. "Why I do believe this is Wally T. Meecham's paycheck?"

"Why do you think Miss Parsons wants us to stay here? Why don't we just go on to Wally's and be done with this silly business?" Melinda asked.

"The question is, will we be finished with this business if we go? Maybe your Mr. Meecham is harmless as you believe. But I don't think you are as sure of that right this minute as you were when he first showed up here."

"No, I'll have to admit that I'm a little afraid right now."

"Well, in that case, don't you think that you are in a better position right now than you will be at some later date when you're alone and don't have the protection that you have in place right now?"

"Yes, yes, I guess that makes sense."

"I shouldn't have to remind you that Miss Parsons is no fool. She is not going to do anything rash or foolhardy. If I know her, I'll bet she's putting together a plan that will have all the bases covered in case Meecham tries to harm you. Meanwhile, just to be safe, we'll keep a sharp lookout ourselves. You stay here by the phone and keep an eye on the front. I'll cover the back."

"What about me?" the boy asked.

"You just stay where you are and keep up with the time. Let us know the second one hour has passed. That would be 12:02 is that right?"

"12:01," the boy corrected.

Chapter 40: The Plan

The voice on the other end of the line surprised Melinda. "Oh, it's you, Mason." Alice and Jubal listened to several "Yes, we are all right," and "That's right," and "Yes, we will" type responses. When the phone was passed to Jubal, he responded similarly. Finally, Miss Parsons came on and asked to speak first with Melinda and then Alice Coley.

The boy knew from what his father told him that the original plan was being changed. Alice hung up the phone and said that they were to stay put until everything was sorted out by the brain trust of Parsons, Amater, Scott and Dunbar. Before Meecham showed, Jubal was thinking, "I could do worse than hang out with Alice Coley and Melinda Brandon all day." But now that the boy's double dream had come true, he was far from thrilled. He was stuck here now and there was nothing he could do about it.

The three were to stay inside Melinda's house and wait for yet another phone call from Miss Callie. This call was promised before two p.m. The purpose for this delay was to allow for (1) Wally Meecham to be found and put under surveillance (2) Miss Callie, Mason and Sheriff Dunbar to get to Mr. Amater's office in Centerville (3) The police in Centerville to be contacted and briefed. If anything went awry with any of these arrangements, one of Mr. Amater's agents, a person known to Alice, posing as a taxi driver would park his cab in front of Melinda's house exactly at two p.m. That agent would then call for his three passengers at the front door and drive them to the North State Agency office in Centerville.

However, a phone call verifying that everything was in place would also mean that the taxi would not be needed. A call from the Parsons brain-trust would also give Melinda the go-ahead to call Meecham.

"What do you think the Centerville police will do?" Melinda asked.

"I really can't answer that," Alice replied, "because none of us know exactly what we're dealing with here. So far, Mr.

Meecham has merely acted a little strange. He hasn't broken any law that I can think of. And secondly, Miss Parsons is acting on a hunch or theory, not on hard evidence. I simply don't know how the Centerville police will react to all this, but my guess is that we're on our own on this one."

"And I'm crazy enough to go along. I've a good mind to call Miss Parsons up right now and call this whole thing off," Melinda stormed.

"I think you'll have to wait a few minutes for that, too," Alice responded. "Right this minute, I assume that Miss Callie is on the road, that is, on her way here to Centerville. In the meantime I urge you to think twice before quitting. If you give up now you will probably wonder about that decision for the rest of your life. Nobody is going to do anything to Mr. Meecham as long as he stays in line. If everything goes according to plan, and you and he get along, then no one will be the wiser. But, if you want us to leave, just say so, and Jubal and I are gone."

The boy thought he heard saint Melinda say an ugly word, but maybe he was reading his own mind. Alice Coley made a bold speech, but it was also one that could have cost her her job. Apparently however, it worked.

Melinda replied, "You're right, Alice. I'm acting like a stubborn sentimental fool. I want to find my husband's killer more than I want my own life. There is nothing in this for Miss Parsons and everything in it for me. I'll do my best to see this thing through even though I have my doubts, and besides I'm scared half to death."

The boy brought the lofty conversation back down to earth by asking, "What's for dinner?"

Melinda looked at the clock. "You're right, Jubal, it is well past your mealtime. I'll fix us some sandwiches. There's soda pop and ice tea in the refrigerator, and I could make some coffee. Which would you prefer?"

"What kind of sandwiches have you got?" Jubal wanted to know.

"I tell you what," Alice said to the boy, "while I keep an eye on the neighborhood, why don't you go with Mrs. Brandon and help her bring the fixings in here. Each of us can make our own sandwiches, and Melinda can stay close by the phone." Both women used first names for the first time.

At 1:22 p.m. the phone rang. Melinda was told that Wally Meecham had returned to the post office after completing his rounds. From there he went to the City Diner, where he ate lunch."

"From the City Diner," Miss Callie reported, "Meecham drove directly to his home. He's there now. Two of Mr. Amater's men will be watching his every move. If he leaves his house, he will be followed and you will be called. Everything is in place. You can call Wally Meecham any time now."

And to Alice Coley, Miss Callie said, "I found out through my bank connections that Mr. Meecham made a significant cash withdrawal from his account only two days before the locomotive explosion in Fallston. That tells me that the odds of Meecham being our man just went up a few notches. So be extremely careful and don't hesitate to use force if the need arises. Keep the part about the bank withdrawal to yourself. I don't think Melinda can handle that news right now." Alice also had sense enough not to tell Jubal about the withdrawal. If Jubal Scott knew now what Alice knew. that boy would be half way to Fallston without looking back.

"Do you think I should call right away?" Melinda asked.

"The man is supposed to have a terrible toothache. By waiting, giving him a little more rope, maybe we'll find out if he's telling the truth. I'll bet that if you wait until say four o'clock, he'll tell you that he's just come from the dentist. You'll know that that's a lie. I suggest that you wait until four."

"Great," Jubal groaned, "this thing is never going to end."

"You're right, Jubal," Alice said as she stroked his hair. "Detective work is not as much fun and glamour as people make it out to be either in the movies or books. Most detective work is just plain waiting. And then waiting some more. Then tomorrow you get up and do the same thing all over again. But if we keep waiting long enough and digging deep enough we're going to solve some of the cases we're working on. If I didn't believe that, I wouldn't be in this business."

Somehow the three survived the strain of waiting until 3:55 p.m. Alice picked up the phone and called her office. "Melinda is making the call now," she said and hung up.

"Melinda cleared her throat, "picked up the receiver and gave the operator Wally Meecham's number. Moments later she asked, "How's your toothache?" There was a pause while Meecham answered.

"I'm glad you finally got up with Dr. Glassman. I know from experience that a toothache is no fun. I hope the aspirin helped." Another pause.

"By the way, I found a letter addressed to you mixed in with my letters. Somehow you left your letter on the table in my den." Pause.

"Yes, as a matter of fact it is an official-looking U.S. Post Office envelope."

Meecham's voice must have picked up a couple of notches, as the boy heard him say, "Thank the lord, woman, I left you my paycheck. Thank you, thank you. I've been looking everywhere for that letter. If you're going to be home for the next ten minutes, I'll be over to pick it up. I have something very important to talk to you about."

"Yes, I'll be here," Melinda answered. There was another pause. During this pause, Melinda became visibly upset. Nevertheless, she managed to keep her voice under control long enough to say calmly, "I was about to get in the shower right this minute. Why don't you give me, say thirty minutes or so, and then you can come over and we'll talk.

"OK. See you in half an hour. Goodbye."

"What's going on?" Alice prompted, as Melinda was giving them only body language, wringing of her hands and the shaking of her head.

"He says he has something very important to talk over with me, and, I didn't like the tone of his voice. It was very uncharacteristic of the Wally I know, or at least thought I did."

"Is that it? He didn't give you any hint as to what he wanted to talk with you about?"

"No. I'm glad I put him off for half an hour at least. But I don't know if I can get myself together by that time. I don't even know if I can get myself together in a day."

By this time Alice was reporting to her boss Mr. Amater and Miss Callie who was also on an extension phone in Amater's office. "Melinda is pretty well shook up right now. I'm not sure how to handle the situation."

Either Miss Callie or Mr. Amater must have dropped a bombshell, causing Alice Coley to gasp, "Are you sure?" She talked for three more minutes and hung up.

"Dr. Glassman has not seen Wally Meecham today," Alice announced.

"How do you know that?" Melinda asked.

Mr. Amater had Dr. Glassman under surveillance ten minutes after I called Miss Callie around ten this morning. No one even close to Meecham's description has been anywhere near Dr. Glassman since that time."

"You know you're not making me feel any better," Melinda complained. "What am I going to do? I'm a music person, not an actress. I'm not sure I can act anywhere like normal."

"Listen, Melinda," the younger woman counseled the older one, "all you need to do is be yourself. The fact that Meecham lied about the toothache is not proof that he is in any way involved in the case. He may just have a crush on you and needs an excuse to see you alone. Remember, you are a very attractive woman. I doubt if any woman in this state today has a gentleman caller with so many people watching. Jubal and I will be right there on the other side of that wall in your bedroom. If you need help, we'll know it. Additional help will be right outside. You'll be perfectly safe. Just be yourself."

Melinda took the precaution of changing clothes. As she returned to the den, the phone rang again. "Meecham is on his way," was the message.

Chapter 41: The Showdown

Alice and the boy watched from Melinda Brandon's bedroom window as Wally Meecham parked in front of her house. He parked the car carefully and lawfully, making sure his passenger side tires were snugly against the curb. Meecham then got out of the car and walked around to the passenger door. Next, he carefully removed a large object from the front seat. It was obvious by its size and shape a painting or picture. The picture's subject was covered with a bed sheet or similar type of cloth. "Oh, so that's what he's up to" the boy whispered. "He's bringing her another painting." Jubal was immediately and severely "shussed" by Alice, reminding him that there was to be absolutely no talking, no noise of any kind.

Moments later Melinda and her guest were talking in the den. "I have a painting I want you to see, and I want you to tell me what you honestly think about it. Is it a deal?" Meecham asked.

"All right, but first you'd better put this letter of yours in your pocket. I wouldn't want you to have to come after it again."

"Oh, I wouldn't mind that at all."

Alice and the boy exchanged glances. Even the boy recognized a low pitch like that.

"Is this a new painting, or have I seen this one before?"

"No, you haven't seen this one. I not only want you to see it; I want you to have it."

There was a quiet interlude while both Alice and Jubal guessed that the picture was being ceremoniously unveiled.

"Oh, my goodness," Melinda gasped.

"Don't you like it?"

"Well, er--I--er just don't know what to say. How? Why? What is this all about? I don't understand."

"I painted it from a photograph I found of you in last year's college yearbook. You do like it, don't you?" Meecham's voice was beginning to take on a frightening note now. Alice must have thought so, too. She removed the pistol from her handbag and motioned for the boy to move away from the door.

"It isn't that I don't like it, Wally, honest it isn't," Melinda said. "You've done a wonderful job with the painting, and it was sweet of you to flatter me this way, but I just don't understand why you've gone to all this trouble for me, that's all."

"Don't you see, I did it because I love you, Melinda."

Upon hearing that, Jubal made a brave step toward the door. Alice motioned for him to stay put.

"Listen, Wally, it isn't that I don't appreciate your friendship. You're a very sweet man and I am very fond of you, but right now I'm not ready for any kind of man-woman relationship. I'll keep the painting if that's what you want, but only under one condition. And I want to make that condition perfectly clear. There is absolutely no romantic attachment on my part implied by my accepting it. Is that understood?"

"Just give me a kiss, and I'll give you more time to think about it." Meecham was demanding now.

"No. A kiss would serve no good purpose for either of us. It would be best for both of us if you leave right now. We've been friends a long time, Wally. If you leave right now, that relationship can and will continue."

"No! Stop, you're hurting me! Please."

It must have been in that moment that Wally Meecham realized that all his desperate, bloody plans had ended in failure. He knew in that instant, that he would never have her, at least not in the way he'd dreamed about. Wally Meecham's reaction to Melinda's rebuff was violent and swift. Meecham yelled, "You ungrateful bitch."

As Melinda Brandon screamed, Alice Coley grasped the door knob.

"What kind of a life did you have with that killer you were married to? Everyone knows he killed that man at the railroad shop," Meecham continued.

With the door snatched open the boy could see that Meecham was gripping one of Melinda's arms. With the other hand he'd snatched a heavy black object from a nearby shelf. The boy recognized it as one of a pair of antique flat irons Melinda was using as bookends. Hers were exact replicas of the type Aunt Sarah still heated on the wood cook stove and ironed

228

the Scotts clothes. It was clear that Meecham meant to smash Melinda's head with the three-pound chunk of wrought iron.

Meecham's target, however, turned out to be elusive. Melinda managed to twist away from Meecham's first swing. As he righted himself for a second swing a bullet from Alice's gun smashed into the fleshy part of Meecham's upper arm, the arm holding the flat iron. Wally Meecham dropped the iron, let go of Melinda's arm and turned to face Alice Coley in disbelief. "Hold it right there, mister." Alice instructed the startled mailman.

By then, the boy was on the phone in the bedroom. "This is an emergency. Get me the North State Investigation Agency quick!" And, within minutes Melinda's house looked like the site of a police convention.

Chapter 42: Later

Later that afternoon, police discovered a gun in Meecham's bedroom. That gun eventually proved to be the one that killed Albert Caswell and pumped bullets into the wall behind Aunt Sarah's stove.

Meecham was convicted of killing Caswell. He also confessed to the murders of Brandon, King and Spencer at Fallston. Lacy Brandon was killed with a blow to the head with a steel pipe as he stooped to throw the spur track switch, which would have allowed the empty flatcars into the siding.

Meecham was about the same size as Brandon, and wearing Brandon's cap, was able to get inside the cab of the locomotive and hit Spencer over the head before Spencer suspected anything. Only George King was alive at this time. And King, with his arthritis was no match for the agile killer.

By the time Caswell arrived at the engine, the crew had already been killed. Caswell shut off the locomotive's water supply valve beneath the tank tender, cutting off flow into the boiler. Then he opened the manual drain valve beneath the locomotive and emptied the boiler onto the ground. While this was going on, Meecham realized that people were nearby at the barn. He then sent Caswell to keep anyone from coming to the dead locomotive. While Albert Caswell was holding Jubal Scott and bargaining with Frank Ruffin, Meecham dragged the body of Lacy Brandon to the locomotive and placed it in the cab with the the other dead crewmen.

With the final placement of bodies, Meecham called Caswell. Caswell was undoubtedly horrified to find three dead bodies in the cab. But it was too late to do anything but what he had already been paid to do. He closed the manual injector valve and looped one end of his one-hundred-yard coil of rope around the horn of that valve. With the injector valve closed, Caswell could safely reverse his earlier procedures without getting killed himself. He closed the boiler water drain and opened the main water supply under the tender tank. Then carefully trailing the rope behind them, the pair headed toward their getaway car.

231

The rope was arranged is such a way that pulling on the rope would open the manual injector valve, while at the same time moving the injector valve handle from an upright to a horizontal position. As the handle moved from vertical to horizontal the loop was expected to slip off. It was a tricky maneuver that Albert Caswell could only hope would work on the first try. Caswell gave it a mighty yank. Cold water rushing into the cherry red belly of the boiler did the rest. Luckily for the killer and his accomplice, the loop end of the rope was free. Caswell and Meecham quickly recovered the rope and fled. They got away, but not for long.

Wally Meecham paid for his criminal acts with his life in the gas chamber at the North Carolina State Penitentiary. He died as the sun came up on the ninth day of August 1943. His death fulfilled Frank Ruffin's prophesy that dragons die at dawn.

Melinda Brandon eventually recovered from her ordeal and ultimately became Jubal's stepmother. Mason and Melinda were married on Christmas Eve in 1942, the Scotts moved into Melinda's home in Centerville; Jubal became a city boy.

Jubal's father managed to convince the Yankees who owned the farm that Brodus would make them a good overseer. Brodus and Dove moved into the big house. This meant that Aunt Sarah and Uncle Frank did not have to move.

When the big truck loaded with the Scotts' belongings was ready to leave for Centerville, Mason Scott was taking one last look. Aunt Sarah noticed Jubal leading his two stick horses across the yard and away from the house.

"Where yo' headed wid yo' hosses, honey? Yo pappy's looking fo' you. He says he's bout ready to go. Why don't you take yo' horses on over to his truck?"

"I'm gonna turn em' loose," the boy said sadly without looking back.

"Why you gone do dat, seein' as how you love dem horses? And dey's yose."

"Riding horses don't belong in no town, that's why."

Jubal continued along the path to the packhouse. Tears were now streaming down Sarah's cheeks. "Dat po chile."

232

At the packhouse the boy eased the halters and reins from the necks of Vinegar and Veedeevoo and tossed them atop the pile of tobacco sticks. Now they looked for all the world like all the other tobacco sticks.

"Hey, Jube, are you ready, son?" Mason called from the front porch.

"Here I am, Papa. Yes, sir, I'm ready now."

Miss Callie Parsons' part in the drama cannot be overstated. Without her financial support and forensic insight, Melinda Brandon would likely have become Wally Meecham's next victim. What did Callie Parsons get for all her troubles? For her time and money? Miss Callie Parsons got sheer enjoyment and blessed assurance that God does answer prayers. In addition, the name of the Fallston Baptist Church was changed in later years to Parsons Memorial Baptist Church.

The sudden death of Callie Parsons in 1946 appeared to be the end of Fallston. Modernization and technological changes in agriculture were rapidly making large farm families unnecessary and obsolete: The era of labor-intensive farming was over. But the town simply refused to die or disappear. Following the end of World War II, plants of another sort began to spring up in the area: textiles, pharmaceuticals, garments, food processing and lumber plants. The state began to open technological schools. Displaced farm workers could learn the skills required to grow the new plants, maintain their livelihood in an industry that is continuing into the twenty-first century.

Now, thanks to renewed interest by private citizens and grants from historic preservations societies, the old mansions on Fallston's Main Street are being restored. The State of North Carolina is also rebuilding the old fort on its splendid site overlooking the river. There, a dozen Confederate cannons have recently been plucked from the bottom of the Roanoke River. These will eventually be restored and reassigned to guard duty on the cliffs above Fallston's bend of the Roanoke. There are rumors that a band will perform a concert in the newly refurbished Fallston city park next summer.

In order to establish seniority, Mason Scott began work at the Centerville Railroad Shops as a pipefitter. In February of

233

1943 he enlisted in the army where he served until the end of the war.

Throughout the war years farm labor was in short supply. It was not unusual in those days for city kids to spend their summers working on Eastern North Carolina farms: Jubal Scott was among them. What made it unusual in the case of Jubal was that Brodus and Dove let the boy keep his old room. Jubal Scott may have been the only white boy on an all black operated Eastern Carolina farm those summers. The summer of 1945 was Jubal's last on the farm. Four years had passed since the explosion at Fallston. Uncle Frank was no longer able to share the tobacco curing duties with Jubal. Boots was now a regular primer, leaving Jubal to do the trucking.

On August 10, Jubal's last day on the farm. Melinda was scheduled to pick him up around seven p.m. The boy rode Cindy from the river barns to the stables, where he released her into the company of the other mules; time now for her to kick up her heels and roll in the dust. But instead, there were giant tear drops in the huge animal's eyes. Cindy seemed content just to wander around as if looking for someone or something. The boy did not have to wonder who or why. Frank Ruffin had not been to the stables since Chester died six weeks earlier. There was no doubt in the boy's mind that Cindy would eventually get over the loss of her two friends. But the task which now lay before the boy was the most difficult one he's ever faced-- saying goodbye to Uncle Frank. The family had been told the old man was slipping away. Maybe a day. Two at the most.

The boy took his time washing the tobacco gum from his hands. Boots, Thad and Brodus were there, but very few words were exchanged. Causes to celebrate would have been easy to name: the war was over, last day in the field, the prospect of high prices for this year's tobacco, and a plentiful harvest. But even if the people on the farm had known that they were gaining the whole world that summer, they still would have known that they were losing the very soul of the place.

A few minutes later Jubal blew his nose, wiped his eyes and made his way to the foot of Frank Ruffins bed. The old man, his snow-white hair emitting the aura of a halo, appeared to be sleeping. The grief stricken boy was about to make his way out of the room when the old man spoke. "Come heah Jube where Uncle Frank can see yo."

"You know that I'm going home tonight, don't you, Uncle Frank?" It was a stupid thing for Jubal to say, but the boy had lost all self control.

"I'ze gwine home tonight, too. Did you happen to know dat?"

"But you are at home Uncle Frank. This is your home."

"Naw, son, yo Uncle Frank means dat he's gwine home to be wid de Lawd tonight."

"No, sir, you're going to be alright. You're--"

"Now hush yo fretin', boy, Uncle Frank's done talked wid de angels in glory. Dey say's deze 'xpectin' me.

"But I don't want you to go Uncle Frank, I love you."

"I love yo, too, boy. But I got to go. I ain't no mo' good heah. Yo'd sooner have Uncle Frank happy in glory wid his Lawd and Savior 'dan layin' in'dis heah bed, now wouldn't yo?"

"I guess so, but I still don't want you to go. I'll come back to see you every chance I get."

"I know yo'd do dat, but dey ain't gwine be no need. I'ze gwine see yo every day from now 'till yo comes where I'ze a goin'.

"How are you going to see me every day from where you're going if you're going to heaven?" Jubal was struggling to understand what Uncle Frank was saying.

"Yo go to yoh Bible and see what hit say's deah in de book of de Hebrews 'bout dat cloud of witnesses. Dat's where yo Uncle Frank gwine be. And when yo gets in trouble or weary 'long de way, or gets lonesome, or when yo wants to give up, yo jus' listen out fo' Uncle Frank. He's gwine be a' watchin' yo from dat cloud wid all dem witnesses in it. Uncle Frank gwine be be a shoutin' to yo Jube,-- C ome on boy, yo can beat dat thing dat's a' botherin' yo."

Aunt Sarah entered the room and took the weeping boy into her arms as she had done so many times before. "Come on honey, Miss Melinda's heah. Yoh Uncle Franks' powerful tired right now. We got to let him rest.

235

Jubal's beloved Uncle Frank Ruffin died quietly in his sleep later that very night.

Jubal's terrible sick headaches continued until modern technology came to his rescue. Allergy tests, finally led physicians to the cause of Jubal's headaches. and medication became a godsend to Jubal's headaches in his adulthood.

Chapter 43: The Flag

Patrick Mercer loved fishing, but the man could not abide snakes. That same Patrick Mercer was buried on the first day of December of 1999. Pat lived to the ripe old age of ninety. As a young married man Patrick and his bride found themselves living in a small house by the railroad shops in Centerville, North Carolina. At the time Patrick made his living driving a truck for a large produce company, hauling produce to and from the rail head in Centerville. When his wife inherited enough money for the couple to relocate in the snakeless fishing part of the country, Patrick jumped at that opportunity and never looked south again.

Patrick was able to use the company truck for his move. A co-worker who happened to be vacationing near the town where the Mercers were moving agreed to pick up the truck and drive it back to Centerville. Patrick Mercer looked across at the sprawling railroad shops one last time. The shops were touted as the biggest passenger car repair facility on the East Coast. But Patrick knew he would never work there again.

Suddenly Patrick felt the urge to take something from the giant railroad shops for no better reason than to prove to his children that he had been there. He stood facing the near empty marshaling yard which stood between him and the main repair buildings. There was a fence in disrepair and beyond it something that might just fill the bill. There was a red metal flag half buried in the summer weeds. Near the flag sat a dilapidated rusty, paint peeling passenger coach. Patrick's first thought was to grab something out of the old coach. But for his purposes that would be both too risky and time consuming. So he quickly worked himself through one of the spots where the fence was vulnerable to anyone wanting to cross it. And watching carefully for snakes for one last time, he reached for the flag. He expected to yank it out of the ground, only to find that it had been spiked into a solid cross tie instead of the soft ground. Having gone to this length, Patrick was not to be outdone. He wiggled and twisted the flag until it gave up, and the prize was his.

Sometime later, Jack and Curt, Patrick's sons, cleaned out their father's garage. They rented a Dumpster to dispose of everything they considered to be trash. The house had to be emptied and put up for sale.

Jack is the older. He had the final say.

Curt, the younger and softer of the two, was questioning his brother's seemingly heartless indiscretion on almost every item. "Hey, what's this doggone thing?"

Curt had tossed that sentence at his brother one time too many and his patience was near the breaking point, but luckily the garage was almost empty. "What thing are you whining about now?"

That thing you just threw in the Dumpster, Jack, that red metal sign. Pop must have wanted to keep it for some special reason. What do you think?"

"You're probably right. Pop probably did have a reason for saving it at one time, but I doubt if we'll ever know the reason why."

"Look Jack, the word "PIPEFITTER" is printed on it, and look here, Jack there's more. There's more! It has "Property of Atlantic Coast Line Railroad" stenciled on the back of it."

"So?"

"So what are we going to do with the thing?"

"We're gonna do what Pop shoulda' done years ago.

"Yeah, and what's that?"

"Where is it now?"

"It's in the Dumpster right now. You know that."

"Well, my advice to you is the same advice I would have given Papa years ago."

"What's that?"

"Leave the blasted thing right where you found it. It's gettin' late. Let's get outta here."

William M. Davenport
E-mail bwilliamd@aol.com

About the Author

William Davenport grew up on a tobacco farm on the Roanoke River in eastern North Carolina. The farm was located very near a town that had once been a thriving river port. Davenport's father became the overseer of a struggling tobacco farm during the Great Depression. On that farm, while yet a young child, Davenport received hands-on training in the labor intensive business of tobacco farming. While in the midst of the intense struggle for the farm's survival, young Davenport also learned much about the struggle between good and evil. In the nearby village where Davenport attended church and school, the boy became fascinated by the many colorful reminders of past glory he found there. There, on farm and town the seeds of "Dragons Die at Dawn" were planted.

Later, as a young man, the author hired on as a railroad pipefitter's apprentice where he learned that trade and worked on the last of the steam engines and the first of the diesels. After serving in the U. S. Air Force during the Korean War, the author used the G.I. Bill to foster his college education. After attaining a master's degree from East Carolina University in 1963, he began a new career as an aerospace engineer for NASA at Goddard Space Flight Center in Maryland. He retired from NASA in 1995 at the age of 68. While writing as a hobby, several of the author's articles have appeared in major magazines including Reader's Digest and Guideposts. The farm, river port, locomotive and tobacco horses were real. The rest is fiction.

DATE DUE

			MAY '07

9 781588 201225